# Lost Decency

# Lost Decency

## The Untold Afghan Story

## ATTA ARGHANDIWAL

Library of Congress Control Number: 2012907132
All rights reserved worldwide
ISBN: 978-0-615-55758-8

Cover and interior design by Lydia D'moch
Front cover photos: *(top)* © by Qudsia Arghandiwal;
*(bottom)* © by Yusuf Rafiqzada
Back cover photo: Pro Image Studios

Printed in the United States of America

*To my late brother Ziaullah,*
*a courageous freedom fighter who revolted against*
*local communists and the Russian army for over ten years.*
*He ultimately lost his battle with cancer in February 2010.*

# Contents

Գեզ Գեզ Գեզ Գեզ

# Lost Decency

# Russian Chocolate

REMEMBER, YOU ARE GOING to Russia tomorrow, so go to sleep," shouted my mother as she prepared my clothing for a "big trip" to Russia. Although it was true that we were not going to the heart of the "iconic" Russia, or very deep at all within the borders, sleep was the last thing on my mind. In the morning, we would be crossing into Russian territory at the natural border through Amu Darya (the Oxus River), which makes up about eight hundred miles of the Afghan–Russian border. I was excited about the adventure but also apprehensive about its possible dangers. As one of eight children at that time, I wasn't quite as sure as my father that I was the "lucky child" whose turn it was to accompany him on his trip, but I knew it was meant to be an honor.

I had earned my day trip over the border, and it was quite an accomplishment in my family to be selected. My father had been assigned to a four-year mission to establish and foster improved military relations with his Russian counterparts as Afghanistan's central government commissioner in Imam Sahib, a border town located in the northeastern part of the country, in Kunduz Province. My father had a difficult choice to make every time he journeyed into Russian territory, and it was always predicated on his children's being acceptable companions and able to avoid any embarrassment. I must have behaved awfully well, because I could tell that he was particularly excited to share the trip with me.

I was always curious why my mother did not accompany my father on his frequent trips, but one of my brothers broke the ice by inquiring, "But, Mother, you never get to go to Russia. How come?"

"Well," she said, "women are not supposed to travel and be amongst strangers in strange areas. Besides, I can't go to Russia with a veil on my head." She laughed as she thought of it. "It would be quite a scene for me to follow your father covered from head to toe," she continued.

Surrounding my mother now, we asked more. "But, Mother, why do you have to wear a veil still?" my older sister insisted. "What about this new freedom for women?"

"Well, the new rule is very exciting for the Afghan women, but I think it is still too early," my mother said with a smile. "I will hopefully go to some places without a veil, but Russia is not one of them. Maybe someday."

Breaking through the gang surrounding my mother, my father shared news that dramatic changes were on their way as a result of the newly elected prime minister, Mohammad Daud. My father was especially optimistic on that particular day, as there had been a spectacular "shedding of the veil," along with other promised social and economic changes that echoed a new, modern age for Afghanistan. It was 1959, and we were all excited about the future.

My father was the government's highest-ranking military official in Imam Sahib, working alongside a high-ranking civilian official responsible for the overall control of the city, with extended authority to the outlying areas. My father was responsible for the overall security of the area, which included at least six border posts alongside the Amu River, as well as a large military contingency stationed in the heart of the city. Aside from his military tasks, he was also responsible for communication and negotiations with Soviet military officials on their side of the militarized border, on behalf of the Afghan government.

My father was not only a very powerful government official but also very well respected and liked by both local and Soviet officials. I remember his calm demeanor and professionalism as we traveled to the Soviet Union; I felt very proud to be his son. He had a sense of discipline and a professional air about him that were obvious to his men and to me, even as a child. To be a part of his preparation and talk surrounding his trip was awe-inspiring, and I knew I wanted to be just like him.

The long night passed, and my internal clock woke me in the dark of the early morning, when we had to leave in order to board the ship for a short trip across the Oxus River to the shores of Russia. Afghanistan's border with Russia is separated and marked mainly by the mighty Oxus River, navigable for over eight hundred miles.

Respecting the serious nature of the trip, we drove by car silently through bumpy unpaved roads during the early hours of the morning, through heavily wooded areas leading to the border area in preparation for our journey across the river. Awaiting our departure was a Russian military ship, and I sat glued to my seat, unable to communicate and in awe of the power I was witnessing firsthand. The medium-size river vessel left the dock with us on board and cut through the Oxus River as if nothing could stop it. The mighty river would overflow and cause massive destruction during the rainy season. It seemed stronger than the river itself, and it gave me a chill that I would remember always. Even in the presence of my father, I had never felt so small.

The intensity of the two-hour drive and boat trip to the Soviet outpost was palpable, and it is obvious now that my father's preparation for those trips was to steel himself in the face of a storm that he could not predict but was charged to defend against if necessary. As a child I had no real grasp of the powers at play. My schoolmates and I were constantly taught and lectured about Russian communism as if our identity had already been predetermined. It was not only the words "Russia" and "communism" that clawed at me. But, like the feeling I had crossing the river, those two words somehow instilled in me conflicting emotions of fear and curiosity.

It always seemed odd to me that as a Muslim nation we studied the nature of Russian government and communist ideology, which clearly was contradictory to our beliefs. We considered the Russians to be *kafirs* (non-Muslims/infidels), yet we were embracing their government not as if it were a lesson in political science, but as a sort of awkward cultural exchange. Little did we know, the map was already being redrawn, right under our feet.

In a matter of minutes, we were standing on Russian territory, but I turned back for a brief moment, thinking we'd traveled across the greatest ocean imaginable. I was afraid now, but I knew from my father's teachings that I could not show it.

While the soldiers and officers greeted us kindly, with broad smiles, it was hard to overcome the fear I kept hidden inside. My hand began to tremble as we were escorted to our quarters, where I was separated from my father and his two Russian companions. I was led outside the military headquarters to play with other children.

At first we were unable to communicate, but our commonality was soon established in the form of a plastic soccer ball, and we found ourselves engrossed in an impromptu match. After a couple of hours, we children were asked to join the adults, and I was delighted to hear that the hearty meal would include Russian chocolates.

Finally, the meal ran its course and the long wait to get hold of these chocolates ended. They were indeed tasty, and my fear had subsided enough to enjoy them without worry; the pure enjoyment of an amazing treat was all I could think of.

As another hour passed, I was reluctant to hear the news that it was time to prepare for our departure after such an exciting day on

*Myself (third from left) with two of my sisters and my two brothers a week prior to my trip to Russia with my father.*

Russian soil. It seemed as though all my fears had been for nothing, and these intimidating Russians were just people like me, but with amazing chocolate. When I learned that we would be taking back bags of Russian chocolates with us, so that we could share them with other Afghan officials and their families, I almost lost control with joy and had to catch myself just before I felt my father's icy stare. The scarcity and lack of availability of foreign imports in Afghanistan made these types of treats almost irresistible to everyone, especially the children. It was an innocent time of wonder and possibility, and it seemed maybe that we had a good friend in the Russians after all.

As we departed, bags of chocolates in tow, we saw no real signs of tension and danger with Russia, and Afghanistan, though isolated, did not lack for basic needs. Filled with budding friendships, life in Afghan society was simply peaceful and relatively untouched by the West and outside influences. Other than my trip across the border I honestly cannot remember any particular tension or concern about our neighbors to the north. The majority of Afghan people maintained a very simple but healthy lifestyle. Due to my father's prominent position with the military, our family enjoyed an excellent standard of living, and the kingdom and government were stable, well respected, and supported by the country as a whole.

# Impoverished Kingdom

ᘓᕄᘓᕄᘓᕄᘓᕄ

Bᴇᴄᴀᴜsᴇ ᴍʏ ᴘᴀʀᴇɴᴛs ᴛᴏʟᴅ ᴍᴇ ᴛᴀʟᴇs, starting in my early child-hood, about being part of a kingdom, it felt like a huge honor and source of pride, and I found images of kings quite intriguing. In Afghanistan, the king was the greatest source of power and authority, besides God and the Prophet Mohammad, with whom we associated our lives. Every Afghan knew the king's status.

At the time, Mohammad Zahir Shah ruled the kingdom, a self-proclaimed monarchy his father had established. After gaining its independence from Great Britain in 1919, Afghanistan had gone through amazing modernization efforts under the former king Amanullah Khan; during his ten years in power, he had initiated dramatic changes in both foreign and domestic politics through his new relations with external powers, and had transformed domestic politics with his social, political, and economic reforms.

Although Amanullah's reign ended abruptly, he achieved some notable successes, and his efforts failed as much because of the centripetal forces of tribal Afghanistan and the machinations of Russia and Britain as because of any political folly on his part. But unfortunately extremists and fanatics had seen his efforts as pure westernization and strong opposition, and they forced him to abdicate power in 1929. Amazingly, glimpses of Amanullah's progress, such as the rail system and Qasr-e-Darulaman, his palace, remain even as we speak.

After a brief civil war, a tribal assembly chose Mohammad Nadir Shah as king. During his four-year reign, he restored peace while continuing some of Amanullah's modernization efforts at a more moderate pace. He was later assassinated in 1933 and succeeded by his son, Mohammad Zahir Shah, who then ruled Afghanistan for forty years, even though he effectively shared power with his uncles and a first cousin, who served as his prime ministers.

King Zahir Shah was born in Dehradun, British India, his family having been exiled following the second Anglo-Afghan war, and was educated in a special class at Habibia High School in Kabul. He continued his education in France, where his father had been sent as a diplomatic envoy, studying at the University of Montpellier. When he returned to Afghanistan, he helped his father and uncles restore order and reassert government control during a period of lawlessness in the country. He was later enrolled at an infantry school and appointed a privy counselor.

King Zahir Shah was only nineteen years old when he assumed the throne in 1933. But over the next twenty years, the monarch let his uncles run the country and slowly open it up more to the outside world. In the 1950s, Cold War rivalry drove Afghanistan's development agenda, as the Soviet Union and the United States tried to outdo each other in offering aid. Moscow paved the capital's streets, constructed municipal buildings, and built the Salang Tunnel. Washington responded with a highway across southern Afghanistan, an international airport in Kandahar, and an ambitious irrigation project in the Helmand valley. The United States turned down several requests for military aid, after which Kabul turned to Moscow and received a wide selection of tanks, fighter jets, bombers, helicopters, and small arms.

Following the end of World War II, King Zahir Shah realized the need for the modernization of Afghanistan and recruited a number of foreign advisors to assist with the process. Also during this period, Afghanistan's first modern university was founded. However, a number of the king's potential advances and reforms were derailed as a result of factionalism and political infighting.

Despite these issues, King Zahir Shah was able to rule on his own in 1963, and he proved to be a firm but gradual modernizer. The proof came in the 1964 constitution, the most liberal the country had ever seen. It set up a constitutional monarchy with a bicameral parliament. It also turned Afghanistan into a modern democratic state

*In Imam Saheb, behind my father, while watching an Independence Day celebration parade.*

by introducing free elections, parliament, and, although framed in an Islamic context, a secular legal system that included equal rights for women and freedom of expression. Although these changes were not popular with Islamic traditionalists, it was truly a golden age.

All these efforts were characterized by a lengthy span of peace, but not enough to satisfy the Afghan people. The king was a feudal master who for the most part was considered to lead a life of luxury while the majority of his people lived in substandard conditions compared with other nations with a similar history of independence, such as Japan.

For the last five years of his life, Mohammad Zahir Shah served as a very ineffective and fragile symbol of unity for the country he ruled for four decades. Under his leadership, Afghanistan was neutral during World War II and pursued a diplomatic policy of nonalignment. In reality, King Zahir Shah was a peaceful man and did not like to get involved in politics; he would rather enjoy painting, reading, and simply enjoying his luxury life, even as the majority of his people were deprived of basic education and access to better living standards. He remained largely a figurehead, rather than an effective leader, of an innocent nation that would suffer dearly as a result of his incompetence during his reign and years of war and occupation.

King Zahir Shah was ultimately overthrown by his cousin (prime minister at the time) as the result of a coup d'etat in 1973 while he was in exile in Rome. He chose to abandon his throne rather than provoke bloodshed, and moved to Italy, where he lived in exile for twenty-nine years in a modest four-bedroom villa, spending his time playing golf and chess and tending to his garden. He was barred from returning to Afghanistan during Soviet-backed communist rule in the late 1970s. In 1983, during the Soviet war, he was cautiously involved in plans to head a government in exile, but ultimately those plans failed because he could not reach a consensus with the powerful Islamist factions. In typical fashion, he elected to enjoy his time in Rome, similar to the time when he had ignored the possibility of Afghanistan's war with Pakistan when he was king.

Despite Zahir Shah's actions, Afghanistan was still beautiful and peaceful. People simply went about their business and enjoyed their untouched traditions. That's right—great traditions were the cornerstone of every Afghan and of society in general.

I still vividly remember King Zahir Shah's black Chevrolet speeding through the unpaved streets of Kabul as kids chased the car and cheered, until they could no longer see through the dust he left behind.

# Seeking Prosperity

$\omega\wp\omega\wp\omega\wp\omega\wp$

AFTER HIS EXTENSIVE AND GLORIOUS military missions around the country, my father started to get tired of travel and wear and tear from the military lifestyle. We were a large family with eight kids, and that was a concern for him, as he had realized the need for better education for us. He therefore requested early retirement from the army in order to return to Kabul. After many attempts and extensive lobbying, his wish was granted and he began a new career, working for the department of transportation.

Our family started a new chapter of life in the Afghan capital. Kabul was starting to grow fast, with tall modern buildings nuzzling up against bustling bazaars and wide avenues filled with brilliant flowing turbans, gaily striped chaps, girls wearing skirts, well-dressed men, schoolchildren, and a multitude of handsome faces and streams of whizzing traffic. New residential areas with modern architecture were starting to form in various areas, particularly in the newer parts of the city.

Kabul was surrounded by mountains gleaming emerald green in spring and glistening white in the winter, and by ever-changing beauty in the fall. Kabul River used to flow through a narrow pass between the mountains and through the heart of the city. Travelers from all around the country were captivated by Kabul's charm. As a true crossroads and center of trade, political turmoil, and more, the capital had many great sights to visit, such as mosques, several famous gardens built by past rulers, museums, mausoleums, ancient walls, and citadels.

The words *Kabul* and *Kabuli* echoed and registered as a matter of pride, even for a child. While the people of Afghanistan took great pride in their birth cities in various corners of the country, moving to Kabul or even visiting the capital city remained a dream of every child. With over 3,500 years of history and as the largest city in Afghanistan, Kabul was the country's most popular and attractive destination, not only to locals but to tourists from all over the world. It was home to many empires, valued greatly for its unique strategic location, for its scenic beauty provided by hills and gorgeous mountains, and for its status as the nation's cultural and learning center.

Contrary to some people's undeserved portrayal of Afghanistan today, which may lead others to assume that this is all Afghanistan has ever been, the reality is that the Afghanistan of the past enjoyed amazing peace, some progress, and a sense of privacy, and was well on its way to better days.

Afghanistan was also noted for its brilliant poetic languages, which its great poets used to inspire many by writing messages of humanity, equality, and unity. We were also very proud of our female poets, such as Rabia Balkhi, Rabha Adawee, and several others. From the 1950s through '70s, music and radio were becoming commonplace around the country, and with the introduction of several orchestras featuring Afghan and Indian instruments, as well as the emergence of music idol Ustad Sarahang, Afghan classical music was starting to gain recognition not only inside Afghanistan but in the surrounding countries as well.

For our parents, education remained the top priority and the great equalizer. Despite the limited availability of schools around the country, the main focus of every child was to attend college someday and even earn a scholarship outside of Afghanistan, thereby securing opportunities to advance the standard of living. While some schools were more suited to provide education for the nation's elite, there were opportunities for others to attend local elementary and middle schools. In all cases, children were expected to turn in good grades.

In those days, Afghan women were starting to pursue careers in various fields, including medicine. Contrary to today's harsh conditions, no one had to worry about any violence against schools. Afghanistan was enjoying a solid tradition of law and order, with a government capable of taking on some national infrastructure projects, like building hydropower stations and roads, with help from foreign governments. Every ordinary Afghan had a sense of hope and belief in a bright future through education, which the government had actually improved between 1933 and 1973 by making primary schools available to about half of the population younger than twelve years of age and by expanding the secondary-school system and Kabul University, established in 1932.

As a result, women and men in the 1950s and '60s were starting to look for careers in various fields after their graduation. I remember going to Kabul University's campus during my middle-school years; it was a truly promising and motivating scene that every young adult dreamed of being part of someday.

# Lost Decency

After seeing and being attracted to the university aura, several friends from school and I started to look for ways to just get close to the campus. One easy way was to take advantage of sporting activities. Our parents knew soccer and volleyball in particular were being played on university campuses and at a few other schools with facilities, so we had their blessing once in a while. Looking at the pictures today, I am reminded of the amazing feeling that I had at the time, knowing that I would attend a university someday.

As students, both young women and men wore Western-style clothing; girls' schools in particular used to provide beautiful uniforms. We were never allowed to wear traditional Afghan clothes in school. It was all about business and professional attitudes. The habit of wearing pants and Western-style clothing was even spreading around the other big provinces and cities of Afghanistan.

No one knew that all that promise and the opportunities the innocent children of Afghanistan currently had would soon turn into despair.

# Shahrara
# (Our Safe Haven)

DURING HIS PROVINCIAL COMMISSION DAYS, my father asked our uncle to purchase a home for us inside the capital city. Our uncle bought this home in an established area called Shahrara, which is located northeast of the city, right below hills that are home to a military garrison overlooking a large residential area. The house was located off the main unpaved road connecting the old neighborhood from north to south, which extended about four miles in length and two miles in width, with a historic tower called Burj Shahrara in the south and Bagh-e-Zanana (a women's park) in the north.

Shahrara was in many ways very similar to other established neighborhoods of Kabul, with homes within compounds, built mainly from mud bricks, with a few exceptions made of sun-baked brick or cement, and attached to each other with narrow alleys separating them every few hundred yards. The majority of the homes were two stories and had several rooms in order to accommodate large families (averaging seven to ten children). Our house had a nice-size yard located in the middle, and a big, two-story wall that served as a tower and allowed us to watch people passing by. Besides mud walls, though, nothing else seemed to separate the community.

Most rooms in our house were furnished with large Afghan rugs and had little space for storage; we did not have too many things. The guest room on the second floor was very nice, decorated with a beautiful rug covering almost the entire floor, a few portraits of our grandparents, and even some posters displaying a minaret and the popular highway and high mountains that connected the west and east and led to Pakistan. This room was to be used only by guests and for sleeping purposes. My younger brother and I were the lucky ones who were allowed to sleep there. We would simply move our mattress and blankets into the room every night and remove them in the morning.

The big house included two bathrooms and a large, detached kitchen with several typical handmade wood-burning ovens. The bathrooms were big enough to bathe in occasionally, but most of us preferred to use the neighborhood public baths *(hamam)*. The *hamam* were quite popular, especially the newer ones, which provided private rooms for a higher price. Going to the public baths was particularly a treat in the winter; for parents of eight children, it was not an easy task to provide heating and water every day, so our bath at home was never comfortable and warm enough to enjoy. Plus, there was always a wait. It especially felt great during harsh snowy days to get up early for a good bath and get ready to shovel the snow off the rooftops and home alleys and walkways. Ah, and the best part was buying sweet beet right at the doors of the *hamam*. That served as the best energy bar ever.

Our neighborhood was similar to others within the big city: It seemed to be a self-sufficient little territory containing many small stores within a few yards of each other, each selling different items with little competition. We had a bakery, a butcher shop, a grocery, and even a couple of small *samawars* (teahouses), which offered limited menu items, such as rice and soup. Most of these areas with wider roads, even in residential areas, turned into little bazaars that would come to life in the early-morning hours and stay open until dark.

As an older and more established area of the capital, Shahrara was very crowded indeed, a true melting pot where branches of various ethnic groups lived together without any threat. Everyone had an enormous amount of respect for each other. People within the neighborhood knew each other very well, and no one from the area was considered a stranger. We of course put first our father, mother, sisters, and brothers, but all adults were referred to as *kaka jon*, meaning "dear uncle," or *khala jon*, "dear aunt," which was amazing. Children were not allowed to use the word *kaka* or *khala* by itself; *jon* ("dear") is traditionally an automatic extension to names indicating respect. One did not have to be old to be called *jon*, though— just older.

As children, we spent the majority of our time at school, doing homework, or playing outside, but only younger girls were allowed to play alongside boys outside; older girls could not mingle with the opposite sex. With the exception of school or official work, these girls had to stay home and help their parents with daily chores.

Women and children spent the majority of their time within these walled compounds, while men ventured into the outside world for work in the city. It was an uncomplicated way of life, without any major hassles, and I honestly cannot remember knowing anyone who was ever alone during that time. People were simply surrounded by family and friends. It also felt like we were actually brought up and parented by more than our natural parents; neighbors and elderly people took care of us as if we were their own children. They would stop us from behaving badly and praise us for what we did right. We lived in a "we" environment where everyone was responsible for each other's well-being and happiness.

Our daily lives within this close-knit network consisted of the basic human elements of living: listening to stories that were often repeated, helping with household chores, eating together, walking to school together, and caring for each other outside of the home. Boys' daily assignments varied from the girls'. Boys participated in chopping wood, bringing home groceries, taking *khameer* (bread dough) to bakery shops, and oftentimes carrying wood, charcoal, and water. Oh, yes, getting water into the house was probably the biggest challenge of all. During the early days in many of these neighborhoods, water pipes ran only through the main roads, with public faucet locations spaced half a mile apart. Digging water from wells and carrying it home was a major task for many boys.

In later years, people who could afford to pay had the option of extending water pipes right through their homes, but the first and best option was to have water delivered by *saqao* (water carriers) who used sacks made of animal skin and delivered water to houses all day long. The job of the water carriers must have been one of the most difficult and challenging occupations ever, as these workers carried water to homes on surrounding hills and upward to the hilltops and mountains that ran through and surrounded most of Kabul.

Still, the boys had the big advantage and the freedom to roam around. Besides homework and some other chores, we spent a lot of time outside the home compound, playing, mingling with friends, and flying kites. Kite flying and pigeon flying were the most popular neighborhood activities. Skilled pigeon handlers and kite runners surrounded the entire area. Pigeon flock owners would fly their flock mostly in the morning. Hundreds of colorful pigeons were trained to fly above and around our home area, with the ultimate goal of attracting someone else's pigeon to join them. The owners would then identify and capture the pigeon and tie its wings for a few days, sometimes weeks, in order to train it and acclimate it to its new surroundings before untying its wings. Attracting and capturing someone else's pigeon was a big personal challenge, oftentimes causing personal conflicts and fights within the neighborhood. But it was a fascinating game, not only followed by pigeon flock owners, but by hundreds of spectators watching from their rooftops and windows.

During the weekends the skies in Shahrara would be lit up with colorful kites; a few owners just loved to fly kites of various sizes and colors for fun, but most owners were preparing for competition. The object was to cut someone else's kite in the air using crushed-glass threads that could rip the opposition's kite threads. The outcome depended on the level of expertise and the price of the thread used to cut the opponent's kite. People would also place bets on such games.

Our favorite activity, though, was just getting out of home confinement and playing with neighborhood friends. Playing soccer on dirt and even in tight alleys was our absolute favorite, along with *toop danda* (hitting a ball with a stick), which was similar to baseball but with very few structured rules. For a long time it was almost impossible to find a true soccer ball to play with, so we had to resort to very popular but cheap plastic balls imported from the Czech Republic and other Eastern European and Asian countries. That was the ideal ball to have, since we could use it to play both soccer and volleyball.

While women throughout the country did not have much freedom, they were vehemently protected as the most honorable group within our society. There just seemed to be an amazing standard of respect and care among members of this community. Aside from school, girls spent most of their time at home cooking, embroidery, cleaning, and babysitting younger siblings.

I also remember my sisters' asking our parents for permission to join the Girl Scouts. Boy Scout and Girl Scout programs, similar to those in the United States and European nations, were being formed, with hundreds of students from elementary and middle school enrolling. But when my siblings and I asked to join, our parents rejected the idea, as they believed we were just too busy and the program would distract us from our education.

*High school years with members of the Boy Scouts (second row, sixth from left, with my brother Zia standing second from left).*

Eating meals as a group was a big tradition and way of life for many Afghans. Everyone sat around on large, colorful cushions called *toshak*. These cushions were normally placed on the colorful handmade rugs and carpets for which Afghanistan is famous. A large cloth or thin mat called a *dastarkhan* was spread over the floor or carpet before the dishes of food were brought in. In summer, food was often served outside in the cooler night air or under a shady tree during the day. In the depth of winter, food was eaten around the *sandali*, the traditional form of Afghan heating, which consists of a low table covered with a large duvet called a *liaf*, big enough to cover the legs of the occupants sitting around the *sandali* on their cushions or mattresses and supported by large pillows called *Balesht*. Under the table was a charcoal brazier called a *manqal*. The charcoal inside had to have been completely burned previously and well covered with ashes.

Food was usually eaten communally; three or four people would share one large platter of rice and individual side dishes of stew *(qorma)* or vegetables. Homemade chutneys, pickles, and fresh *nan* bread usually accompanied the food.

The traditional way of eating was with the right hand, and with no cutlery, although spoons might be used for puddings, and teaspoons for tea. Because hands were used in eating, there was a hand-washing ceremony before meals using a special bowl and jug called a *haftawa-wa-lagan*. Younger boys and girls were responsible for carrying these items around to all members of the family.

While this was respected as a tradition, it is fair to say that it was also the most difficult and hated household job of every child in Afghan culture. Being part of a big family and network of close relatives meant that one child would have to carry this job out for a group of twenty-plus at times. Just imagine carrying the two-piece hand-washing utensils around and watching every single person take their sweet time washing their hands! My younger brother, Zia, and I had the honor of carrying out this responsibility, but because of our one-year age difference, this task always caused huge arguments between us. As the older brother, I expected him to do the task, but he did not like the idea; he thought of this assignment as a demeaning habit and family expectation, and he would constantly resist or simply run away, so I ended up washing hands more than he did.

Eating together as a family was the most intriguing and amazing quality of Afghan culture. Not only was it an established tradition that made things easy for mothers, but the gathering reaffirmed family unity—and it was also an opportunity to pray together before and after every meal.

# Two Mothers and Faith

ᏗᏇᏗᏇᏗᏇᏗᏇ

$M$Y FATHER HAD TWO WIVES. In the Islamic tradition, men could marry more than one woman, as long as it was for a valid reason. I remember asking my teacher during my high school years why it was okay for Muslim men to have more than one wife. I was told that since the early days, men had used their physical power to control, subjugate, and mistreat women, and that men would get what they wanted without thinking of the woman. Women were oftentimes treated like property—hence, to give respect to women, Islam accorded them the status of legal wife so that they and their children would have inheritance rights and a secure future. In most cases, the second and third wife lived within the same compounds as the first.

My stepmother was not able to bear children, but my father greatly desired a big family, so he made the decision to marry a second wife, my mother. Still, my stepmother was an adorable, nice woman who loved us all just like her own. She was much older than my mother, so, in accordance with tradition, all of us, including my own mother, respected her.

# Lost Decency

It is hard to even imagine and compare the lifestyles and traditions of the past with those of the present. Our love and affection for our stepmother was contagious and enjoyed by all. Any different feeling would simply not have been acceptable to my father and mother. Our stepmother was actually the authority figure, next to my father, within the family. She was respectfully granted her own room, with all the appropriate accommodations, and lived within the same compound with peace and dignity while respecting and loving all members of the family. She participated in all home chores and served for the children as a protective soul. We would all run to her and seek refuge in times of trouble and need, as she would protect us from being penalized. Being able to stay in her room was quite a treat: she would tell stories and, most importantly, take care of us with amazing grace and kindness. She truly was a source of inspiration, stability, and strength within our big family.

At this same time, Islam had been established as the official state religion of Afghanistan; it spread from the Middle East through Iran and ultimately extended to Pakistan and various parts of India. Today, approximately 99.7 percent of the Afghan population is Muslim; about 80–89 percent practice Sunni Islam and belong to the Hanafi Islam school of law, while 10–19 percent are Shi'as who follow the twelve branches. A smaller number of Ismalis have a few influences from Sufism that may exist among both Sunni and Shi'a communities.

Since the ninth century, Islam had been established, respected, and practiced in its purest form, without any controversy. Fair to say, Afghanistan at the time was one of the purest modern Islamic societies, where we never heard of hands being cut off or an adulterer being stoned to death. Our grandparents and parents, along with members of all communities within the country, demonstrated the utmost respect and faith and taught us about all the beautiful qualities of a great religion that brought so much honor and fostered amazing chemistry within families and society in general. We would pray along with our parents whenever we had the chance.

The most desirable ablutions for men were the prayer rituals performed inside neighborhood mosques. Every neighborhood contained several mosques, built by communities and well maintained, typically by a mullah or caretaker. Most of the mullahs lived within an adjoining compound built for them.

These mullahs would perform group prayers and also provide Quran lessons to children during the day. So going to the mosque was not only a good deed but also provided an opportunity to meet neighborhood friends and spend time outside the house. I remember spending long hours mingling and at times playing sports after prayers. But no one actually forced us to pray; people who did not participate would simply stay quiet and respect others as they attended to their rituals.

Embracing Islam and religion was a big piece of Afghan life, similar to other Islamic communities around the world that taught people to believe in God, respect, not lie, be fair, lead a selfless life, and, most important, live and work together as one. That was the best form of Islam! It brought so much goodness to us, as everything seemed to move smoothly through its positive and peaceful influence. I am blown away by what has become of religion today.

I cannot remember pondering Islam during those days—as a matter of fact, we never had to. The focal point of Afghanistan's national identity and the basis of its overriding culture and values is the religion of Islam; Islam is both the national religion and its most decisive unifying characteristic. Islam's concept of community *(umma)* has superimposed itself on ethnic diversity and provided the main focus of loyalty. Any social change and development had to embrace this concept to be effective in the short term.

One of the most gratifying and important occasions that united Afghan communities throughout the country was the month of fasting (Ramadan) and its conclusion of Eid (joyous occasions of celebration). During Ramadan, Muslims around the world abstain from eating, drinking, and sexual relations from dawn to sundown for thirty consecutive days. Fasting is intended to teach Muslims about patience, humility, and spirituality. As the month in which the first verses of the Quran were revealed, Ramadan is believed to be an auspicious month for God's revelations to humankind.

Like all other Muslim nations, our entire nation would prepare for and observe Ramadan every year. Children ages twelve and up were expected to fast the majority of the time. Even younger children would join the occasion simply as a matter of pride in and respect for their religion, family, and community. With dinner as the big meal of the day after sundown, Ramadan was also the month for cooking the finest possible food, consistent attendance at daily prayers (five times each day), and going to the mosque for recitation of Quran and its verses after dinner. Society in general enjoyed a more peaceful time and harmony during this month, in which time people were encouraged to refrain from arguments, fights, causing harm, and committing any other sinful acts. Government and businesses would normally close early in observance of Ramadan, so it was the workers' favorite time, as the entire month was considered the laziest one of the year and slowed down the entire country.

Fasting started with a meal before sunrise. This time was the absolute favorite of children, as it would involve delicious traditional snacks prepared and served even to younger children who did not have to fast. Parents and families with younger children wanted those children to remain sleeping so that the older family members could enjoy their early meal peacefully, but to no avail. We kids would be too excited, and would find a way to get up and join the feast. My younger brother, Zia, was a heavy sleeper, so he would always ask me to make sure I woke him up for early-morning snacks, which I did but got in trouble for; still, it was a big thrill for the two of us as we enjoyed our treats while giggling and having fun.

The long fasting days, particularly in summer, passed at a very slow pace; most adults would take a good long nap during the day and in between prayers. While women were mainly responsible for food arrangement in Afghanistan, even men and younger children would help during Ramadan. I remember spending hours at times helping my mother and sisters with tasks like getting the fire started in the kitchen, and wrapping and preparing traditional *bolani* (dumplings) and other popular snacks preferred during the holiday.

All members of the family would anxiously wait for *adhan*, the Islamic call to prayer and time to break fast. *Adhan* was generally broadcast through speakers (when available) from big mosques' minarets or loudly, from open areas of the mosques, by mullahs and volunteers. At least a couple of hours before *adhan*, the elderly and women would relax and listen to Quran or actually read it. The bazaars and shops buzzed with people buying fresh groceries, bread, and snacks. It was a fascinating time, and one filled with joy and happiness.

Younger boys preferred to stay outside and mingle with friends to kill time. We would then wait for the countdown every day and run toward home immediately after *adhan*. Little kids would recite the *adhan* to announce instructions for breaking fast. Everyone would pray together, break fast with a little appetizer/snack, and then pray together again, either at a mosque or in small groups at home, followed immediately by a big dinner with the entire family.

# The Road to Responsibility

᭡᭢᭡᭢᭡᭢᭡᭢᭡᭢

WHILE OUR MOVE BACK to the capital was a huge success and brought much joy to the family, we were abruptly faced with surprising and devastating news. My father arrived home a little earlier than normal one day and wanted to sleep more. I could not remember ever having seen my father sleep during the day, as he was always busy, so we kept on asking our mother why our father was sleeping now. At first she explained that he was simply tired, but later she admitted that my father looked pale and had been holding his left arm tightly.

"Why isn't he going to see a doctor?" someone asked my mother.

"He believes it is nothing serious, but he has promised to go see a doctor," she said.

Later that day, we noticed that our father had completed his afternoon prayer but remained sitting in his place on the prayer mat. When he had sat there for several minutes, we knew something was not right. "We have to take him to see the doctor!" one of us said.

Similar to other South Asian developing countries at the time, Afghanistan faced challenges with regard to the availability of emergency health services. In the early 1950s and '60s, close to half of the people had access to some basic level of medical care. There were only three doctors that covered the big Shahrara district at the time, and all had their medical offices inside their home or adjacent to their property. The doctor closest to our home, Dr. Kandahari, was a great man and a very close friend of my father's. Since we did not have a home phone at the time, I was asked to run over to the doctor's house to inform him about my father's condition. He asked right away if we wanted him to come to our home or if my father was well enough to walk.

"I just wanted to make sure you are available, but let me go ask," I told the doctor.

"Absolutely," he said.

When I arriving back at home, I found my father walking, but slowly.

"*Agha jon* ['Dear Father'], Dr. Kandahari is home and has no problem coming over here," I informed him.

"No, it's better to walk," he said.

The doctor's home and office were less than a block from our home, so one of us accompanied my father there. Dr. Kandahari had turned his second-floor guest room into his medical office, right above his house's main entrance, and he saw hundreds of the neighborhood's patients there. I helped my father climb the stairs to the office, where Dr. Kandahari greeted him warmly. The two men had a great mutual respect, so we knew my father was in good hands.

After some initial tests, the doctor informed my father of some irregularities in his heart and immediately referred him to the central hospital of Kabul. Within a few days of his going to the hospital and undergoing tests, we found that our father had some serious heart challenges and was ordered to avoid going to work immediately.

This was the hardest decision for my father, as he was the sole bread-winner of a big family, which, including my stepmother, had by then grown to thirteen members. But after a couple months off, he regained some strength and decided to go back to work, as he knew he could not afford to provide for all of us on his limited retirement income, with no other obvious source of money except for the profits from a supply of wheat and some other products from farmland we owned in Arghanday.

The good news, however, was the fact that Afghan citizens' greatest asset had been their confidence and self-reliance throughout its history. Being in debt was unusual, even for the poorest among us, while repaying debt and providing a favor for anyone in need, not only within family circles but in society in general, was seen as an obligation and a point of pride. While our family did not have any debt, maintaining our very comfortable standard of living was a huge concern for my parents, especially in light of my father's serious illness. At one point, my mother advised my father to seek a loan from a friend for medical treatment in India, and was met with much resistance from him. It was probably the first time my parents ever had to think about borrowing money from anyone.

"No, I am going to be okay and I will continue to work," my father told my mother.

"What?" my mother questioned angrily.

"That is right. I will get sick even more if I sit home, so I am going to ask to continue part-time," he said. "I will work at least until our two oldest kids finish their education."

That was the first time my father spoke of children's financial responsibility to their family. It was a huge matter of pride and obligation for every father to provide for his family, but in the event of a husband's death, not only would his wife's economic independence diminish, but so would her sense of social protection, so being able to rely on her children, especially male children, was significant.

Despite his serious illness, my father, who was a very determined and faithful man, continued to go to work while taking medication. It was hard for all of the family to see him go through so much difficulty, but none of us was in a position to leave school and/or find work. Our parents remained content to lead us toward completing our education no matter what. We had to adjust to frugal measures in order to make a living now, and it was far different from the lifestyle and spending habits we had been used to in the past, but we still felt very comfortable and it seemed like there was always plenty of food and clothing around.

# Glory Days

In the 1950s and '60s, finishing our school assignments during the day was a top priority for all, due to inadequate lighting in our houses during the evenings. Although most homes within our neighborhood enjoyed occasional electricity, we were faced with consistent disruptions and blackouts. Families during those times would be subject to using gas lanterns and even candles. We would even cuddle in smaller groups to take advantage of lantern light, but with several children inside one house, finishing assignments at home was a struggle.

General education consisted of religion, history, math, geometry, world geography, literature, art, and even sports, despite our very limited access to playing fields for any popular sport, such as soccer. During those times, some parents believed playing sports would slow down the education process for their children and saw it as a distraction; they also did not believe in their kids' straying from their home surroundings, so the kids' going to outlying areas to play soccer was not met with great approval. But eventually our parents accepted it as a normal and healthy activity.

With the emergence of national sporting champions came recognition of Afghanistan's progress from Asia and the international community. There was no TV at the time, so we used to follow all events through newspapers, radio, word of mouth, and even Iranian magazines, published in Persian (with an alphabet similar to our own Farsi). Schools, universities, and even some government and private institutions began forming their own athletic teams. Afghanistan made great strides by introducing and sending soccer, wrestling, volleyball, field hockey, boxing, and track and field teams to other countries for competition, and even the Olympics. I proudly remember Afghanistan's wrestling team's presence at the Olympic Games. We were particularly proud of the few Afghan wrestlers who won gold and silver medals in Asian competitions.

We also enjoyed Afghanistan's national sport, *buzkashi* (goat grabbing). Although the people of Kabul and the rest of the country enjoyed watching it during national celebrations, mainly during the weeklong celebration of independence inside the capital, *buzkashi* is played mainly in the northern provinces of Afghanistan, where horse riding is a heritage of the steppe and fleet horses are raised with pride and care. The game is played on the open plains near towns and villages, mainly during fall and winter. A decapitated calf is placed on a circle before the judges. The object of the game is to pick up the carcasses and ride around a specified point, which might be as much as a mile away, and return to deposit it once again in the circle in front of the judges. The game requires tremendous skill by daring riders atop glistening horses—sometimes galloping flat-out, sometimes rearing with flailing hoofs above an opponent—who make the game irresistibly compelling.

Other popular sport clubs, particularly wrestling, bodybuilding, billiards, boxing, and ping-pong clubs, were opening all around the country. Organized sports were particularly taking shape at high schools, Kabul University, and military academies, and in the air force. Sports were a great escape, as well as a source of pride for the young and old alike.

There seemed to be a very visible level of respect for Afghan people within the region. It may have been the result of their amazing resistance against and defeat of British forces during three famous wars, or because of other instances of the country's resilience and national pride. It might also have been because Afghanistan was identified as a bridge for foreign powers to reach the wealth of India or the warm water of the Persian Gulf—the country had suffered through several invasions over the course of history, and it was the only country in the region to have survived the political oppression of the colonial powers, secured its independence, and managed its internal affairs at the time.

Every corner of the country—its various ethnic groups, customs, ways of life, and even amazing food—used to be admired not only by visitors but also by locals and Afghans traveling within the country. There was a genuine feeling of hope and prosperity in light of Afghanistan's new focus on education and the introduction of women into the workforce. I remember seeing fewer and fewer burqas during those days, as people not only inside the capital but also around the country opened up to progress.

The people of Afghanistan were also starting to enjoy the emergence and status of their nation within the global community, despite poor economic conditions. The country was moving forward as the people looked for dynamic reappraisals and programs. A pride of nationhood was radiating throughout the country, which offered the spectacles of awesome scenery, the excitement of forward movement, and the fascination of a rich past.

As children, we were particularly happy to celebrate and enjoy national holidays, which provided an opportunity for the country to display its talent nationally as well as among other nations within that area. I remember hearing about delegations and guests from various Asian countries during these holidays, such as our weeklong celebration of independence. Afghanistan even designated a special holiday in recognition of Pashtunistan (the disputed Pashtun area between Afghanistan and Pakistan).

There was big buzz about the fact that Afghanistan was beginning to enjoy industrial growth. Foreign embassies and their affiliates were starting to become more and more active, funding various big projects around the country, such as metal shops around suburbs, and textile factories that produced and processed cotton, which held great promise for Afghanistan's economy. The building of the first large hydroelectric station in the early '50s, the Sarobi hydro-power plant, and the development of the Gulbar textile plant—one of the most modern ones in Asia at the time—also took place.

The Soviet Union increased its support for Afghan military training, and more and more opportunities for scholarships and higher education became available outside Afghanistan, particularly in the Soviet Union, Eastern and Western European countries, and the United States; the number of Russian civil and military scholarships mounted into the thousands during that time. By then the Soviet Union had established a very strong presence and influence through the supply of military ammunition and equipment, as well as the education of Afghan military personnel and civilians. The Russians also established and contracted extraction of natural gas in Afghanistan's Sheberghan city, close to the Russian border. The other noteworthy project was a highly complex irrigation and agricultural initiative financed by the United States that would harness the water reserves of Helmand Valley for use by the larger areas in the eastern and southern parts of Afghanistan.

As a result, both Sheberghan in the north and Helmand in the east were becoming semi-European cities, due to the presence of thousands of Russian and American men and women who worked and lived alongside Afghans. Both the Soviet Union and the United States built homes, schools, hospitals, commissaries, and parks within city limits in order to accommodate thousands of workers and families. Even the women there had freedom to move around easily. Afghans in general showed enormous respect and generosity toward foreigners, even to Russian workers and families.

The United States was also trying very hard at the time to become more active and evident in Afghanistan by beginning a student exchange program (AFS), opening a U.S. cultural center in a prominent area of Kabul, and establishing a Peace Corps outpost with hundreds of volunteers. The Peace Corps soon established language training programs, as well as typing and shorthand classes, and hundreds of eager Afghan students within the capital started to attend. Other foreign governments made significant efforts to influence the country, as in the creation of Kabul Polytechnic University by the Soviet Union, the opening of United States Information Services, Germany's Goethe Institute and Amani High School, and the French government's Istiqlal High School, all within Kabul.

Up to that point, we had been very fortunate to enjoy life in a reasonably large house without any fear of financial debt, but the prospect of my father's potential forced retirement and worries about raising ten kids and two wives was starting to take a toll on our entire family. "I want you to go and find out what it costs to enroll in English classes in Kabul," shouted my father one day.

"I know it is very expensive, Father," I responded.

"Go find out right away. I will pay no matter what!" he responded passionately.

I was shocked and speechless. Attending English classes was a dream of every child in that society, but the fact that my father was considering this option for me was a true honor, especially when he was ailing and we were living on a single income. He must have had great hope in my ability to learn English and the fact that it would someday help our family. Within a few days, I enrolled in English classes at United States Information Services, which would open the door to Western civilization and culture for me.

My attraction to learning a foreign language, particularly English, was evident. I had paid close attention to English as my favorite subject during my high school years and had received above-average grades. Going to register and visit the United States Information Services headquarters felt like being accepted to a top university, and it was an event that would change my life forever.

The place was humming with young students and professionals from all over Kabul, although these people were indeed in the minority, as it was very costly to attend these classes. The instructors were mainly Americans and a few Afghan professors. Classes were very different from traditional Afghan schools', equipped with imported fancy chairs and equipment.

The center also had its own big theater, where American residents and diplomats within Kabul could see concerts and movies. The center was a big attraction for Afghan youth and students within the capital as well. It was drawing so many people that it became a real challenge, so the Americans decided to limit entry to the center to students and library members only. But more and more people were applying, and more late-night classes had to be added. The center was indeed a hot spot for those who could afford to pay its high costs.

# Lost Decency

The USIS center was like a second high school for me, a place where I became friends with quite a few students from various other high schools in Kabul and established a group who studied together and spent time together at the center library, in the cafeteria, and outside of school. As our group excelled, we started to benefit from additional classes and materials, including stories from Edgar Allan Poe and other famous American writers.

While attending English classes, we were soon exposed to yet another educational attraction. Within blocks of USIS were the Peace Corps' typing, English, and shorthand classes. I and several of my USIS friends soon joined these classes, which were actually free at the time. Our group started to show great progress there, and soon quite a few of us at the Peace Corps learning center became

*Graduation ceremony from United States Information Services English Language classes, 1973 (back row, fourth from left).*

top students in both typing and shorthand. My friend Asad became the fastest typist, at seventy-five words per minute. I believe he held the record there for quite some time.

All this hard work and interest in English paid off when I and a friend were awarded jobs upon graduating from the center's first-ever sixteen-semester courses. Asad was the first to land a position, as the secretary to the language center director, and I got a part-time job on the center's library staff. This was a rare opportunity and exposure to work during my high school years. Not only was it a prominent location, but along with the job came excellent pay, which was a great boost and source of support to my family, especially in light of my father's deteriorating health.

# The Spartacus Factor

୧ଡ଼୧ଡ଼୧ଡ଼୧ଡ଼

During my last two years of high school (1971–1973), the Afghan people were becoming more and more cautious and aware of the changing political environment. By then King Zahir Shah had ruled for forty years without experiencing any significant war or threat to Afghanistan in general, but his experiment in constitutional democracy had failed him, and foreign powers—particularly the Soviet Union, the United States, France, England, China, Iran, and several Middle Eastern countries—started to accelerate their efforts to increase their presence and gain government and public support.

In light of hopeful but slow progress, growing concern over the state of the country, and the continued dominance of a very small, elite minority, people's frustration in the early 1970s was palpable. Ever-increasing popular opposition to social policies resulted in the emergence of organized political parties within Marxist, Maoist, and even Islamic fundamentalist groups. All these organizations actively recruited many Afghan-educated and government employees while forming groups in rural areas of the country.

As high school students at the time, we started to notice the buzz even within our school, where small groups would start little rallies and demonstrations. Organized antigovernment activities were less visible, and everyone was quite afraid of the consequences. But in a matter of a couple years, demonstrations led by Russian and Chinese communist parties, as well as Muslim groups backed by fundamentalist Middle Eastern groups, started to take shape; more and more people, primarily students, took to the streets, spreading like wildfire within the capital and bigger Afghan cities, and penetrating mainly educated segments of society and the military. It was the true awakening of people in Afghanistan.

Kabul University became the most notable and active place for the launch of organized demonstrations against the government. Crowds of students and interested people would start demonstrations within the university compound, then expand and make their way through major streets all around the capital, ending up right in the center of Kabul's Zarnegar Park, only a few blocks away from Arg-e-Shahi palace.

As high school students, many of us at first had no real understanding of the motive and political situation, and simply loved to join the crowd and march just for fun or as a way to get out of school for a change. But after attending a few rallies and listening to all the slogans and comments of speakers and their leaders, we started to establish a better understanding of the motives and demands for changes. It actually felt good to listen intently and cheer for much-needed progress that resonated with ordinary people's wishes. But it was not fun any longer when the government started to crack down and break up demonstrations, even targeting certain party leaders in order to instill fear and control.

With an enormous push from the U.S., Russian, Chinese, and a few European governments to influence Afghan culture, one of the most exciting developments during this time was an influx of foreign press and arts, which opened the door to the movie industry in Afghanistan. At least seven movie theaters began operating inside Kabul, and at least one or two others sprang up in major provinces. Indian and Iranian movies were the dominant ones, but at least two or three movie showed Western films. We were starting to really enjoy going to movies as a family.

Our parents' approval to go to the movies was a big incentive for children to behave well. At first, men and boys were the first go, but women started to join in, as long as they were accompanied by men. Many of my friends and I were in love with cowboy (Western) movies, especially when they were translated into Farsi, which made them even more interesting and attractive. Next to school and playing sports, movies became the biggest attraction during that time for us. Saving money to see them, even sacrificing food and school allowance to do so, was becoming the norm for youngsters.

While we enjoyed several big movies, such as *Doctor Zhivago,* the most popular one ever to be screened in Kabul's largest theater was *Spartacus.* Upon receiving the news about this megamovie, I and a very good friend of mine, Enayet, who lived a few blocks away from us, decided to run away early from school one day to go see it. After traveling a good few miles on our bicycles, we made it to the Ariana Cinema, located in the popular Pashtunistan Square. Upon arrival, we were immediately informed of the double cost of tickets in order to see the three-hour-long movie. Neither of us had enough money to cover the cost.

"What are you doing?" I asked angrily, as Enayet snatched my new Karakul hat (a style of cap made with pelt, traditionally worn by men).

"Follow me and I will tell you in a few minutes," he said, as he continued running and holding the hat tight in his hand. I was not used to wearing the hat; I had just put it on that day, after receiving it from one of my uncles. Karakul hats were expensive and very popular, and I had no idea what Enayet had in mind at the time. He continued to run toward a street called Nader Pashtun, and that was when I realized Enayet had plans to sell my hat. He was walking and at times running hard toward the hat bazaar and shops located on both sides of the street. I was becoming quite angry and scared as I ran to confront him.

"What are you doing? Give me my hat!" I yelled angrily, trying to grab my hat.

He just smiled, moved the hat behind his back, and took off again. Within minutes, he was climbing the stairs of a hat shop. He turned just as I was about to climb the stairs.

"Stay out! I know this person and will leave the hat as a loan and get it back tomorrow. I don't want my friend to see you! I am not selling it, I promise!" he shouted as he went inside the store.

I was stunned but happy that I would not lose my hat—and, more importantly, I thought it was a reasonable solution to not miss the big show.

Within a few minutes, Enayet was out with money in his fist.

"How much did you borrow?" I asked him.

"A lot! Enough to buy tickets and buy *jalghoza* [nuts]," he said with a big smile on his face.

As we started to walk toward the movie theater, though, I began to feel sick at the thought of leasing my hat to see a movie—what if my family found out? I felt quite unhappy, but Enayet kept on laughing and enjoying the moment. My only satisfaction was the fact that we would be able to see the big movie on opening day, which helped me get over the guilt and anxiety. I was too naive, however, and had no idea until the end of the movie that Enayet actually had sold the hat, probably very cheaply, just to cash out enough money to buy the tickets.

"You idiot!" I shouted at him as I chased to hit him after exiting the theater. As very close friends, we would beat up on each other quite often.

"It was only a hat," he said as we rode our bikes home.

As we rode, we faced demonstrators occupying Zarnegar Park and surrounding the streets right in front of the presidential palace. This was the biggest crowd ever gathered to demonstrate for changes; the people were carrying rebel flags and large banners.

"Wow, it looks just like the movie," I said.

"With no swords yet!" Enayat yelled back as we approached the crowd. It was right around late afternoon and closing time for government and business offices, but the roaring sound from the huge group occupying every inch of the city center made it truly feel like the rebellion of *Spartacus*. Afghans had risen to their feet to fight for the freedom of the oppressed and poor against the incompetent and the aristocrats, right in the heart of the capital and in front of the palace. It was truly a remarkable moment in the history of Afghanistan and this movement, which would ultimately build enough strength to strike fear into the heart of the kingdom.

# The Beginning of the End

᭨᭨᭨᭨᭨

As a result of networking opportunities through United States Information Services (USIS), the Peace Corps, and new people, I was able to connect with a member of the public relations department of the Hotel Inter-Continental in Kabul, who informed me about a sales representative position. I was fortunate to land this job because of my knowledge of the English language and my typing and shorthand skills. This hotel was one of the top five-star hotels of central Asia at the time, with a great reputation.

The Hotel Inter-Continental, built on a hilltop above Bagh-e Bala (High Garden), a graceful, domed palace, officially opened for business on September 9, 1969; it was a subsidiary of the Afghan finance ministry, but was partially owned and managed by Pan American at the time. It served as the nation's first international luxury hotel, and was the one most visited by foreigners since its opening. It had two hundred rooms and was equipped with a nice swimming pool, a gym, three tennis courts, and at least four restaurants. The entire operation was run through the Hotel Inter-Continental's chain management, with a few functions, such as human resources, run by Afghan professionals.

This was a time when Afghanistan enjoyed true peace and was considered one of the top travel spots for Europeans and American tourists. The hotel hosted dignitaries, government officials, and business guests, and was a prime choice for many American and European oil companies' big tourist groups who were looking to stay in Afghanistan. As a matter of fact, the hotel was occupied primarily by foreigners; it offered very limited access even to prominent locals and government employees, who rarely visited its restaurants, swimming pool, and tennis courts.

As a member of the hotel's marketing team, I had the pleasure of staying engaged in Afghanistan tourism promotion, so I not only had to learn about my country but also started to truly appreciate its natural beauty, its costumes, and my ability to introduce many people to its untouched traditions and rich history. Meanwhile, Afghan people's hospitality was further reason for the country to become a favorite tourist destination in the early '60s and '70s; the streets of Kabul and many provinces were filled with travelers from all over the world, who roamed around freely without any fear or discomfort.

The Afghan Tourist Organization was also growing, recruiting and deploying travel agents to places like the Hotel Inter-Continental and other in-demand areas. The organization at the time established an office at the Hotel Inter-Continental, equipped with guides and cars ready for travel anywhere around the country. The influx of tourists from all over the world also provided great sales opportunities for many Afghan women and men attempting to produce and promote various handmade items, clothing, and antique sales across the country.

Hotels and guesthouses were opening at a fast rate throughout the country to accommodate the influx of tourists. Shar-e Naw (New City) and Tora Baz Khan were becoming major tourist destinations, filled with hundreds of accommodations and shops selling antiques, Afghan rugs, and various other traditional Afghan items. The area was even becoming a major attraction for many local Afghans, who were fascinated by the presence of so many foreigners.

But as a result of the increasing influence of foreign governments on Afghan affairs, precedents for parliamentary opposition and student militancy alike were becoming well established. This was an opportune time for various political systems to take shape, especially the foundation of a communist party within Afghanistan.

With over half their trade dependent on the Soviet Union, the Afghans were forced to accept prices that were generally inferior to those that might have been obtained on the world market. By 1971, there was widespread famine, and with relief operations hampered by government incompetence, more than one hundred thousand people died, which only added fuel to the fire.

After all, responsibility for the failure had to be laid at the door of Afghanistan's then-king, Mohammad Zahir Shah. He was generally seen as decent, well-intentioned man who was a genuine patriot and had the best interests of his country at heart. But for most of his reign, he had done very little other than occupy the throne while his uncles and cousins ran the country, and he seemed to never have learned the art of leadership.

While trying hard to exert himself, Zahir Shah lacked the courage and decisiveness to follow through on his proposed reforms to ensure their success. His biggest failure was his constant unwillingness to pass the political parties', provincial councils', and municipalities' legislations, which would have given his government, as well as these groups, the political support they needed in order to function effectively. He had been concerned about the passage of these acts' being gateways to extremism and factionalism. Many believed the king's own son-in-law, general Abdul Wali, warned the king during the 1970s about the danger of a left-wing electoral victory if political parties were allowed to form. Eventually, the king's security—which was in the hands of Abdul Wali, who was responsible for the palace guard and the key army apparatus—failed, and he didn't learn what his cousin Mohammad Daoud Khan (aka Daud) and his supporters were up to until it was too late.

The golden age started to turn red, first politically and then literally, after a bloodless coup d'etat on July 17, 1973, in which Daud seized power while the king was vacationing in Italy. It took very little effort for Daud and his supporters to carry out their coup; with

*With top two national tennis champions (second from left) after a tournament held at the Hotel Inter-Continental, 1977.*

help from only a few hundred troops led by a few officers, they seized the palace and other key positions inside Kabul. They encountered very little resistance from Abdul Wali, who was allowed to join the king in Italy. It is believed that quite a few members of the Parcham communist party actively supported Daud during and shortly after the coup, and there is little doubt that it was only a matter of time before the party influenced Daud's government and expanded its role.

The July 1973 coup put an end to two hundred–plus years of royal control. It was mainly acceptable and pleasing to most progressive movements, due to Daud's leadership and association with Marxist ideology, and the fact that various communist parties had unofficially established themselves with enough public support. Daud was seen by many as a savior and a powerful leader, after decades of millions of innocent people's wasted hope for a viable constitutional monarchy.

After completion of the coup, Daud took over the office of the president, the prime minister, the foreign minister, and the minister of defense, while also assuming control of the central committee, which was composed mainly of military officers. He sent a number of communist leaders to various provincial posts, where their reformist drive was soon stifled by locals and strong hostility. It did not take long before local communists became frustrated and found themselves excluded, and lost their sense of purpose within Daud's government, with the exception of one main communist party, which on principle had been happy about Daud's takeover and had avoided active participation in his regime.

Daud was forced to concentrate much of his energy on addressing growing unrest. He dismissed communist allies and members of communist parties who had penetrated the Afghan military, expecting to share power and eventually get rid of him. He also faced the huge task of dealing with both Islamic militants as they continued their fight against the communist movement and politicians who had served in King Zahir Shah's constitutional government. Many former leaders fled to Pakistan.

Having isolated himself from the liberals who had served the king and from the Islamic militants he had persecuted, Daud had to rely heavily on his security and military forces to stay in power. Still, the Marxists effectively penetrated them. As a result, Daud's efforts to prevent a countercoup were bungled. While most of the armed forces stood aside, Marxist collaborators in the army and the air force overwhelmed republican guards and launched a bloody assault on Daud's palace in April 1978.

# Call of Duty

Just as things were starting to look up for me both from a financial and a career-advancement perspective, I was faced with my biggest challenge to date, next to my father's illness: the decision of whether to join the army or ask for a postponement. Military service was a requirement for all Afghans when they reached eighteen, except for college students, who were required to finish their one-year service after graduation.

This was truly a challenging decision, as I was earning great income while working at the Hotel Inter-Continental and providing support to my ailing father and my family. If I requested a postponement, even with a proper excuse, the maximum time would be one year. After I discussed the options with my father, whose health continued to deteriorate, he advised me to enlist so that I could get the assignment over with and put it behind me.

A month after enrolling for service, I was called to report for duty. My father by then had been hospitalized for a mysterious bleeding problem, so it was an extremely difficult time for our family. Joining the army in Afghanistan was no easy task under any circumstances, as all but the most elite and well-connected draftees had to deal with very harsh and primitive conditions. Despite these subpar circumstances, Afghanistan maintained a strong military at the time, supported mainly by Russian ammunition and equipment, and it instilled fear not only in the eyes of its enemies but in those of its soldiers as well.

Soldiers could be assigned to anywhere around the country, with very limited time off. Only soldiers serving within their local areas had the opportunity to occasionally visit family; many finished their entire one or two years of service without seeing their relatives. Still, military service was probably the toughest and proudest accomplishment of any Afghan.

ⓖⓔⓖⓔⓖⓔⓖⓔ

"Attaullah Arghandiwal, Air Force!" shouted the officer taking roll on my first day of training. Names were read loudly and repeated at least three times. I was quite relieved and a little excited, despite the possibility of being assigned to a remote air base. I hoped to be dispatched to one of the two large, local air force bases near the capital instead. This was just the first hurdle, as we had to go through another, similar process at the air force home base, which was located next to Kabul Airport, about six miles east of the city, in order to find out our permanent area of assignment.

"Attaullah Arghandiwal to Khojarawash, Kabul!" shouted an officer the next day, as we lined up at the air force home base. I went completely numb, filled with relief and happiness. I had hoped and prayed for an assignment in Kabul, because of my father's illness and my concern for my family. I also knew that my father's prayer was being answered, as he wanted badly for me to remain close to home.

Within hours of this announcement, forty-plus soldiers and I arrived at the headquarters of Mahale-Qumanda (Air Force Command Center) located at the northwest edge of the air force base. This center had no walls around it, just an open field behind it, with less than a mile separating the big base from the village. I remember our short walk through the fields to buy homemade yogurt from villagers, who would walk toward the base with their supply.

This unit was very well known for its extreme discipline and tough conditions, which only fit soldiers could handle. I was luckily in very good shape and ready for such tasks as a result of my continued involvement with soccer, which was surely the reason for my assignment with the rest of the group.

My new group and I were officially introduced, handed our uniforms, and quickly led to our sleeping quarters. This area, known as *qaghoush*, was one of the scariest, filled with large groups of soldiers. This command center had two large sleeping quarters, each with over sixty beds. The two quarters were separated by a narrow entryway guarded by a couple of soldiers 24/7. Soldiers traditionally carried wooden boxes with locks, but in recent years many big-city and urban-area soldiers had begun bringing their suitcases. Soldiers were allowed to carry only one case small enough to fit under their *charpai*, a four-legged bed with a base made of woven ropes tied to the frame and four legs. The majority of these beds were squeaky and covered only with a thin standard-issue cushion and blankets.

After we had had a couple hours' free time to get organized and settled, the big whistle blew. It was like the sound of a fire alarm. Everyone started to put on their uniform and to get ready for the lineup. There we were, all 120 soldiers of the unit, lined up perfectly in front of the commander and his assistants. We were first taught the rules of the lineup, the salute, and the discipline required to listen and obey. Right after this big orientation session, it was time for a dinner called *qaran wana*, which means "military diet."

Exactly two hours after dinner, the whistle blew again, and it was time to head to a big room for new soldiers' orientation and initiation. After putting on their uniform in a matter of minutes, all the soldiers were off to the *dars khana* (education room), a big mud room filled with wooden boxes used as chairs, alongside a few thick wooden benches. You had to find a spot to sit quickly, or you would end up sitting on the floor to listen and learn. After reciting every soldier's name and filling the attendance sheet, a captain (often the most veteran and active member of the group) called to the front row a couple of soldiers, who were required to stand straight while looking only at the officer.

The officer then called upon a couple of veterans to step forward and slap the two soldiers. We found out while whispering amongst ourselves that the two had been chosen because of their low voices and low morale while they had recited their names for attendance at the beginning. The two veteran soldiers started slapped these two men repeatedly, until the weaker one fell to the ground and had to be helped to his feet by a couple of other soldiers. The beaten soldiers' faces were completely red and swollen by then. This was supposed to be the first big lesson for all the newcomers. Then it was time for learning other basic soldier duties, followed by a night-time guard assignment, before we were finally allowed to head to our sleeping quarters.

We were informed that basic soldier skills, including gun use, etc., would start the next day, followed immediately by guard duties. As I sat on my bed and tried to sleep, I was reminded of the warning the night before about the training and heavy-duty tasks the next day held, so it was hard to sleep, and I simply tossed and turned the entire night in anticipation and fear, while also worrying about my sick father and how my family would deal with all the challenges.

Around 4:30 AM, we were suddenly awoken by the annoying sound of a whistle repeatedly blown by a solider while standing between the two *qaghoush*.

We soldiers had only minutes to dress and make a quick run to the bathrooms, as we were expected to be standing in line soon, ready for instructions and the start of basic training. It was the end of fall and beginning of winter, with temperatures falling to twenty to thirty degrees at night and in the early mornings. As the soldiers lined up perfectly in two long rows, the whistle blew again, and the commander walked in front of the rows and ordered the *awpashey* (damping and water spray) of all walkways to get them ready for sweeping. The new soldiers were then handed water containers, while the established soldiers were given other cleaning instructions. I and several other soldiers rushed toward the wells, where we had to draw water by lowering a big container and pulling it up using a wooden bar and rubber rope. Each soldier had to take a turn to fill his bucket and carry it for spraying.

I did not realize how incredibly cold it was until I started to spray water through the bucket over the unpaved ground, walkways, and roadways leading to the only paved area of the general command center. The only way to avoid frostbite and pain was to switch hands and continuously puff breaths of air into them, always being careful to avoid being noticed by the veteran soldiers/captains, as they kept on inspecting soldiers and making sure no one was wasting time or moving slowly. We witnessed at least three new soldiers punished by repeated slapping during our early-morning cleaning assignments, so the motivation to move on, do a good job, and stay aware of scare tactics was in the mind of every soldier. It was quite an amazing scene to see hundreds of soldiers hustling while constantly looking over their shoulders in total silence, with only occasional, fearful whispers. That silence was only broken by commanding officers screaming instructions to move quickly and get the job done. This task lasted a good two full hours before it was time for a short break and breakfast.

Our breakfast consisted of a loaf of wheat bread and a cup of tea with sugar, which was never enough to satisfy the needs of a tired body, so soldiers with money would find a way to occasionally buy eggs, cheese, or a glass of hot milk. Breakfast today would be followed by our much-anticipated first full day of training out in the fields, consisting of six hours of drills and other basic exercises.

After these grueling exercises, we finally returned to the base in late afternoon. It was then that I realized why so many soldiers ran away from military service: it was quite easy to understand why some would simply not be able to endure such physical, verbal, and emotional abuses. Although things would get better and easier for some, enduring the first few days and months of military service was quite a challenge and a big test of character for every young Afghan in general. But because completing military service was also one of the highest honors and proudest accomplishments, I had every intention of remaining and finishing, despite the temptation to run away.

Running away from service was not only a difficult task but also a huge embarrassment for the runaway soldier and his family; the soldier would be considered and treated as an outcast and traitor forever. Capture of a runaway soldier would also result in severe punishments, including imprisonment, detainment in wet tents for numerous hours, and continuous low-morale activities, such as bathroom cleaning. Still, when we reported for classroom training the second evening, we found out that at least eight new soldiers had run away and were not present. At least five or six others were quite sick but still had to be present and ready for classroom training.

I was starting to worry—not only about living through these harsh conditions, but also the fact that my father was lying in a hospital bed. But somehow I knew my father's and mother's prayers would be answered and that things would work out. On my third day, while training in the fields, I was summoned by a commanding soldier to report to office. I was shaken and extremely fearful of either getting bad news about my father or being reassigned to a remote area. Reassignment was a common practice as a result of spots opening up when soldiers ran away, so it was a very tense three-mile walk back to the base. As I stood and saluted in front of a waiting base commander, I was told to report to the central command base, less than a mile away.

Being called to headquarters was quite overwhelming. I rushed over there and went through a customary questioning, then was quickly led to the office of air force central training. I was dying to hear what was going to happen; I was very excited to learn that the training center had requested a Farsi typist and the office of deployment had sent them my draft papers, on which they had noticed my Farsi and English typing skills. I was given a Farsi-typing test right away and questioned extensively about my knowledge of both English and typing. I was truly happy to be given a test, as I was quite confident about my skills and typing speed. Not long after, I was told to go back to my original base and wait until my transfer forms were ordered.

Within hours, I was carrying my belongings to one of the most prestigious headquarters within the military, with a guarantee of great military service free from the usual duties and fears. I was no longer just another soldier! After a quick introduction to the members of this thirty-plus-officer unit, I found out that the majority of the officers had received their higher education and training in the Soviet Union, the United States, the United Kingdom, France, and India; quite a few were familiar with the English language and were very well educated.

They were all very excited to hear English, as a few of the active officers were on their way to the United States for high-level pilot training (called squadron at the time), and I was a perfect candidate to help them with their English-learning assignment. Within a matter of days I was acting more like an officer and was treated with much respect and enthusiasm. Within a week or so I was not even required to spend the night at the base and could go home on military buses and return for assignments in the morning.

I no longer had to eat the standard military meal but instead enjoyed the lunches and dinners provided for active pilots and members of the air force education team. It was quite a treat, and I no longer had a feeling of being oppressed but rather a feeling of accomplishment and making a difference. I was very proud to find myself teaching and helping ranking pilots and officers with the English language. I was serving and acting like an officer.

# Communism
# Within the Military

CAN YOU PUT THESE BOOKS in your desk drawer?" asked a high-ranking officer named Said Mohammad as he entered the office, bending low toward me and speaking softly. I had no idea what to say or how to react, as I was only a soldier and was in no position to question him.

"I will tell you later what they are for," the officer whispered. I shoved the small briefcase into the drawer as real fear penetrated into my veins. I shivered and felt sweaty as I quickly realized the officer and books had something to do with antigovernment activities. The officer must have become aware of the news that day about Defense Ministry inspectors' visit to the headquarters and thus was not able keep the books in his own desk drawer.

Imagine the consequences of being caught with communist books in your desk—it would certainly have meant life imprisonment or death. I became determined to not leave my desk and office for any reason, so as not to leave the books unattended, as I waited the long three hours before lunchtime. When the officers departed for the lunchroom, the officer who served as secretary to the air force director remained in the office, came over to grab the bag full of books, and asked me to accompany him to another office, which was about one thousand feet away.

As we started to walk, the young officer—a very kind, energetic, and respectful man—told me that he was a true Afghan patriot and was helping young military officers with their advanced education and training, and that it was against military rules to bring political material to military compounds. He asked me to read the books if I had any interest in learning about other regimes and ways of life. While he was not threatening in any way, he was quite clear about the consequences of breaking secrecy and the code of friendship, and open about the fact that he had established trust and confidence in me through our conversations and learning about me within a short period.

Just as I was starting to feel good about my service and the fact that I was part of an elite group and treated extraordinarily, the fear of being associated with the communist movement sank in. It was a very unsettling situation. As days went by, I started to pay closer attention to Said Mohammad and his relationship with high-level government officials, and I became intrigued by the notion that there was a real level of unhappiness, similar to that of other Afghan social and political environments, within the Afghan military. This particular officer and several of his close colleagues held key positions within the air force and were extremely active; not a day went by that I did not see these officers talk and connect with a new person. In reality, these folks were recruiting new members to communist parties every single day. I am sure this was the case in all government agencies; if they could move and actively recruit members within the military, then recruiting efforts must have been quite fluid within civil society.

Within a few days, my fear had subsided a little, and it did not bother me as long I did not associate myself with any one group or jeopardize my army privilege. I simply went about my plans to accomplish personal and family goals. However, I was becoming quite conscious of the fact that I was witnessing the changing of a calm and quiet Islamic society by the influence of communism. That was a scary thought, but it never truly registered in my mind that political changes would bring so much destruction and despair down the road. I was simply a happy soldier, anxious to get my time done, get on with my life, and potentially achieve my dream of traveling out of the country and even to America.

ؠۏؠۏؠۏ

"This is a big day, Atta," announced Said Mohammad one day, after arriving early and being the first in the office. I asked what was so special about it.

"We are going to get all the important stuff our nation needs," he said.

"What do you mean?" I said.

He came closer and started to whisper. "There is going to be a special report prepared in this building, and we need to make sure we get a copy of it."

I had no idea what he was referring to, but got a feeling it had something to do with secret air force plans and the reports I had been typing over the last few weeks.

"They are releasing the final report and plan of attack in case of an uprising or attack by another nation."

"So listen carefully," said the officer. "I want you to use carbons out of this box only once, and do not destroy them," he whispered.

62

"You are not to use more than three pages, and never use the same carbon again today, okay?" he confirmed with a commanding voice.

"Place each carbon after use in this other box and use a brand-new one for the next pages." he continued. "Do you understand?"

I nodded yes as fear grew and moved within my entire body. The officer informed me that I and Yaqoub (another Farsi typist within the headquarters) would be the only two typists to be used by the visiting inspectors, and that we would be using the second-floor conference room that day.

"Do you understand my instructions?" he yelled to me as I approached him.

I said yes, and immediately followed by asking him if he had been given these instructions just today. After a long pause, he smiled and told me that he had been working actively with many of the antigovernment officers during the last few months and had made quite a few friends.

"The hell with what they think and believe in," he sighed. "We need to do our jobs and get out of here." He sounded very confident and actually quite proud about his relationship with party officers and that he, too, was going to play a big role in bringing positive changes to the future of Afghanistan.

Yaqoub was a few years older than me and had been postponing his service for a good three years, so I looked up to him as a mature friend. But I was very puzzled and actually quite annoyed by this assignment, as I had no idea what this all meant and what the future would bring. I did not want to be associated with any disruptive changes at this critical stage of life, as I had my ill father and family always in mind and simply wanted to get out of the army and help them.

"Go up and don't leave until you are told to do so," instructed the commanding officer at our office. We were then led into the conference room, furnished with a long shiny table with at least ten chairs around it and two typewriters with stacks of paper and carbon-copy boxes. Within minutes we started typing long reports that contained very critical and strategic Afghan air force and ground warfare plans. Frankly, we had no idea what to make of any of the technical verbiage—all we had to worry about was the accuracy and speed to finish each page as we clicked away. Working next to Yaqoub was comforting; we typed for hours, putting away the used-one-time carbons in a separate box and turning over the paper copies to inspecting officers in charge. We used a good three full boxes of carbon between the two of us. Later that afternoon, the assigned officer came in and took the three boxes of carbon away, and perhaps on to the hands of Afghan communist leadership.

"How foolish they are!" shouted Yaqoub as we came down the stairs. "Everyone, including people here in the air force, is sleeping while antigovernment forces are working their way into secrets and building big plans. This is why things are changing: this government is sleeping; they have no clue about all this activity right at their feet."

"Does this mean we now have a role in the government's downfall?" I asked.

"You never know," said Yaqoub as we said goodbye to each other for the day.

A couple months after that day, Yaqoub finished his military assignment and went back to his old job at the ministry of the interior. He was a very smart man; he advised me to be extremely cautious and simply follow Said Mohammad's instructions and never trust any others. I spent the rest of my duty of five months in complete fear, but appreciated Said Mohammad's support and the fact that he never once encouraged me to join the party or execute any further secret assignments. As a matter of fact, he treated me with as much respect as he would a friend, not as an ordinary soldier. I finished my military assignment on time with a big sigh of relief, but also, with a feeling of guilt about having had a hand in some of the biggest potential political changes our country would face.

And while completing that military assignment was the biggest challenge of my young life, my father was not able to celebrate my accomplishment, passing away just months before I finished. Despite his severe illnesses and extended stay at the hospital during, my father remained my biggest supporter and source of motivation to earn this honor and complete what I'd set out to do.

Nothing up to that point in my life had felt more challenging than the tragedy of losing my father. He'd been such an iconic figure and source of stability, not only for his immediate family but for the bigger network of Arghandiwals and the community at large. The thought of his incredible strength, pride, and grace, and the way he cared for his family, children, and others, provided much motivation for me not to give up and to continue to honor him by following in his footsteps and living out the dreams he had for his children.

# Departure Day Disaster

WITH GREAT MOTIVATION and desire to get back to work and serve my family, I returned to the Hotel Inter-Continental after my military service. The hotel had made several new commitments and had booked numerous American, Spanish, German, and French tourist groups, so business was booming.

The two-hundred-room hotel had hardly any openings, and fair to say it was running at 99 percent efficiency at the time. Aside from the tourist boom, the hotel was now also attracting some local wealthy Afghans through special programs, such as tea parties, concerts, and open membership to the swimming pool and tennis courts. Few people were capable of joining because of the high cost, but it was still a big change, and a move toward opening the door to convenience and luxury for Afghans. I worked until very late almost every day, as we were busy with various marketing activities and events for the thousands of tourists flocking to Afghanistan.

Life outside of work was also starting to look better and better, as even more signs of foreign influence were taking shape in the form of several key new initiatives and foreign-supported projects.

However, in light of the very tense political environment, I and quite a few other workers at the hotel started to feel a sense of urgency to pursue the dream of traveling outside the country and, eventually, to America. With a great income and happy lifestyle, as well as very respected social status, quite a few of my coworkers were starting to actively engage in job searches and travel plans—mainly to the Middle East, but also to other Asian countries. Quite a few friends from our English courses also left for England and the United States during those intense days.

The ever-increasing influence of communist parties and growth were more and more visible as various members of opposing groups were arrested and word of communist influence within the army increased. A real crisis began with the assassination of Mir Akbar Khyber, a prominent communist ideologue and organizer, on April 17, 1978. While the person responsible for the murder remains unknown, the most likely possibilities are that it was the work either of Daud's secret police or of communist leaders from the Khalq party. But some also blamed the American embassy and the CIA as the culprits, so a large anti-American demonstration packed the streets of Kabul on the day of Khyber's funeral.

President Daud took notice of this evidence of support for the People's Democratic Party and immediately arrested its leaders by rounding them up and putting them in jail on the night and early morning of April 25–26, 1978. According to confirmed sources, the military command leader of the People's Democratic Party of Afghanistan was given ample time during his arrest to convey his instructions to carry out a military coup.

At this very critical moment, my high school classmate Sami and I were debating whether to carry out travel plans we had been making for months, upon his mother's request that we travel together to

Iran and ultimately to Kuwait. When we went to apply for visas at Iran's consulate, we were asked to wait for a week or two. After some delays, we were told to obtain our visas the next morning.

We planned our trip to leave Kabul via bus to Heart (border city with Iran) and then on to Kuwait. Bus travel was then quite popular, and we of course wanted to see more and visit Iran as well. Our bus was to leave from Kabul downtown at 3:00 PM on April 27, 1978, but first we had the big task of picking up Sami's visa from the Iranian embassy. We had every intention of being at its door right around opening time, ten in the morning. It was an incredibly tense day, not only because of the thought of leaving the country and our families for a big journey but also because there was an anxious feeling surrounding the city in general. I remember our cab driver commenting about the gloomy mood and tension due to the presence of more and more soldiers around the city during recent days and months.

As we approached Wazir Akbar Khan district, where most of the embassies and consulates were located, we started to hear some gunfire and the sound of heavy bombing far away. We naturally became more and more anxious to get the passport and get out, but the cab driver decided to stop the car and refused to advance from that point. We hurriedly started walking toward the embassy, but then had to retreat and duck as advancing soldiers starting firing in the buildings and streets, which were mainly deserted by then. We remained naively determined to reach the embassy, and after a little while hiding behind big trees and shrubs, we started walking toward it again; we were quickly stopped by soldiers with guns pointed in our faces.

"We are here only to pick up our passports," shouted Sami as a soldier pushed him away.

"You are crazy!" the soldier shouted. "Go home . . . everything is closed . . . get out of here."

At that point, the gunfire and bombing erupted all over the city and people began running for their lives. We tried hard to stop taxis for a ride, but to no avail, as cars were speeding and people were simply running away and businesses were shutting down. We had no choice but to start walking toward Shar-e Naw (New City) on the way home. With no access to radio or phone at that time, we were simply stunned and had no idea what was happening; we continued to hurriedly walk, and at times run, while avoiding military and local police cars and personnel. Within an hour or so the entire city was in total chaos, full of the constant sound of gunfire, planes, and bombardments of military bases and important government sites.

We had never witnessed anything like this in our lifetime, as the people of Afghanistan had long enjoyed a peaceful existence without any real threat or danger. As we left the important foreign government embassies and establishment district behind and headed north toward Shar-e Naw, we felt a little more secure, and we ultimately made it to the Shahrara area. But this was our travel day, and so we wasted no time finding a cab—whose driver we had to pay big money to venture toward Jade Maiwand—in hopes of canceling our bus tickets and rearranging our departure from the country. We still could not truly comprehend the severity of events and military action.

After several dangerous maneuvers and shortcuts, the cab driver was able to make his way to the start of Jade Maiwand. As we approached the area, we found the whole large street full of people running for their lives through chaos and noise, with no traffic control, as they just worked to get to their destination.

We realized there was no sense in waiting inside the cab without any movement, so it was time to get out and start walking toward the bus station. After a huge struggle, we approached the office, which was completely overwhelmed by a screaming crowd in total chaos, with no visible person in charge. After a few minutes, a man stood on top of a table and begged people to remain quiet. He was the first person that day who at least gave us a sense of what was taking place. He tearfully announced that a coup d'etat was indeed taking place, asked everyone to leave the area, and made it clear no buses would be leaving but that all tickets would remain valid. As we came down the stairs, a group of people starting rushing upstairs, telling us to remain there because people were getting hurt on the street and being fired at.

We rushed to get out and witnessed an incredibly frustrating scene: people were simply running, surrounded by the continuous sound of gunfire from surrounding buildings and of cars honking to get people's attention as they, too, wanted to get out of the area. The sound of gunfire got closer and closer as we managed to run a good two miles to the center of the city and on toward home. We finally decided to take a chance and hire a taxi if one became available. At that point, we noticed the closure of hundreds of shops and stores, offices, and government buildings. It was a very frustrating experience as uncertainty set in. On the one hand, we were quite upset about our decision to not act sooner and leave the country; on the other hand, it was actually a relief to know we could remain at home and protect our families in this time of crisis and danger.

"I am so sorry to delay your trip, Atta," said Sami, as he put his hand on my shoulder.

"It was meant to be," I told him. "It is all about faith."

I could see Sami was feeling really badly as he continued to walk with his head down, so I felt really badly for him, too.

"If we could only have gotten our passport and visa a day earlier," he went on to say as we kept walking. He knew that I already had my passport and visa ready but had delayed my plan to leave because of his mother's request. But it was time to temporarily say goodbye to Sami as we approached the main intersection. He hugged me tearfully and prepared to walk to his home, about two miles away from the area.

"Get in the car!" yelled a man from inside a taxi. As I looked around, I recognized a good neighbor from Shahrara, so we rushed to the car. It slowed momentarily without coming to a complete stop. I managed to get in the car while it was slowly moving, but it took off with a blast as we started to hear the rumbling noise of military tanks behind us. As the driver got on the way to Salang Avenue, which was the main corridor linking a main part of Kabul to the city center, we found the road to be closed and taken over by tanks and soldiers with guns pointed, while occasionally firing in order to scare the crowd and drive off approaching cars.

Our driver maneuvered the car around toward another street and took off with amazing speed. He told us that it was only a matter of time before all other roads were going to be blocked, so he made several turns to avoid major government, military, and police sites. We felt much safer close to home, as people were simply walking around despite the flow of military personnel. But what was indeed happening? No one had any answers!

# The So-Called Revolution

I FINALLY MADE IT HOME and anxiously started knocking on the main door of our house with much anticipation and anger. My mother, who was visibly upset, guardedly opened the door, then cried and hugged me tightly.

"Is everyone home?" I was mainly concerned about my six sisters at that point. I somehow knew my two brothers would be okay, but getting all the girls home safe was our major priority.

"Three of them are home, but go find the rest," she said.

We felt better about a couple of our sisters, who went to school together, but the youngest one was a major concern, as she went to a school right below the military compound on the top of Tapai Shahrara and no one had yet attempted to go find her.

"Why didn't you go get her?" I yelled.

"We were just waiting for one of you guys to arrive," my mother responded.

The military base was by now a direct target and was being shelled occasionally. The base not only was a major garrison but retained a huge weapons-and-ammunition depot all around the hill, so all

# Lost Decency

Shahrara residents feared explosions and damage. Upon my brothers' arrival, we quickly made a decision to go three different routes to find our sisters. We turned on radios, but one could not hear any live broadcasts, just the sound of commands and military and police forces using various codes and signals.

This went on for hours; we were all intrigued by these sound bites, because it was becoming more and more evident that a major coup was underway. My brother Zia and I went out on foot, taking two different routes as we headed towards our sisters' schools. We were determined to follow the routes they usually used as they walked to school every day. We were filled with a sense of despair and challenge that none of us had been prepared for.

After a couple of tense hours, we were able to unite the entire family at home, and then it was time to find out what was really taking place. It was around three in the afternoon when the main radio station started to play patriotic songs and music. There was no real announcement, just constant play of patriotic songs. By then it was becoming obvious that the coup was led by local communist parties and supporters of Russia. I simply knew it was the work of all those military communists, and I tried to remember the faces and names of the main leaders during my military service year. Throughout the day, there had been no real sign of armed struggle or confrontation, as the culprits had carefully planned their assault on major military and government sources with very minimal or no resistance. The coup leaders must have planned the military uprising quite well, but our fear of the unknown and anxiety about who could be behind all this was quite unsettling.

"The reign of Daud is over, and the patriotic people of Afghanistan are in charge. The era of oppression and class domination is over! It's time for people to take over and defend their homeland from the elite after hundreds of years," echoed an unknown voice. There were still no names mentioned regarding who was now in charge of the military and government, but people had a sense that it was the work of communist parties because the slogans resembled those heard for a number of years during other massive demonstrations.

It was around eight in the evening when a major announcement was made. On the surface, it sounded like a well-coordinated effort by two communist parties led by major military support. All the broadcasts referred to the "Afghan people's revolution." Then came another, much-anticipated, announcement, which talked about the ending of the last remnants of monarchy, tyranny, and power of the dynasty, and further said that all powers of the state now rested in the hands of the "revolutionary council and armed forces." This statement was shortly followed by another announcement, threatening that anyone who would venture to challenge the rulings of the revolutionary council would be turned over to the revolutionary military centers.

We all sat in awe, completely confused, as the voices on the radio talked about the end of tyranny, Nadir Khan, the threat of disobedience, and power being in the hands of revolutionary council. Why would a revolutionary council be afraid of any defiance at early stages? Then we realized the revolutionary forces must be thinking ahead about power sharing between the communist parties, which would certainly create fear and uncertainty; the two major communist parties had never liked each other very much, despite following the same Marxist ideologies.

These hostile early announcements and tone would serve as a fundamental doctrine for the communists as they led Afghanistan into the future. As we listened to the announcer's determined voice repeating the now-familiar revolutionary slogans, his speeches were also filled with promises of loyalty to our homeland, security, fairness, and equal opportunity for all. He then referred to the transition of power to the smaller People's Democratic Party, under the leadership of Nur Muhammad Taraki, who had once been a U.S. embassy translator.

The announcements also repeatedly called for Afghan unity, national pride, and respect for various ethnic groups within our country. There was an incredibly chilly and subdued feeling amongst all, as everyone within our family by then knew that Afghanistan was to be a communist nation and no longer an innocent and democratic Islamic society. Fear and anxiety was visible in everyone's eyes. My decision to leave the country at this time disappeared, and my

*With friends (second from right) on vacation by The Shrine of Hazrat Ali, a few months prior to the 1978 political changes.*

attention now focused even more on protecting my family and staying together. Fear of retaliation, imprisonment, and abuse in a communist state was starting to sink in, while national pride and a sense of independence was starting to run and boil inside our veins.

Despite our big desires for change and prosperity, the thought of going the communist route was simply unacceptable. My feelings about the change from being considered a Muslim to being part of a communist nation was very unsettling, so I made a decision, along with my mother and brothers, to stay in Afghanistan and await the outcome of changes for a while and not leave my family behind in so much uncertainty.

This military coup, by men of left-wing sympathies, was carried out when the civilian leadership were all behind bars, and on an afternoon when the office workers were off half the day, but it was not long before the civilians reasserted their authority. Several members of the communist leadership had been arrested and jailed by Daud's government. The new authority labeled this change the Saur Revolution (after the month in the Islamic calendar in which it occurred); it was almost entirely the achievement of the Khalq communist faction of the People's Democratic Party of Afghanistan (PDPA). This success gave it effective control over the armed forces, a great advantage over its Parchami communist rival.

President Daud was officially deposed and executed during this coup; he and his government were unable to receive adequate support from their well-equipped armed forces. The Democratic Republic of Afghanistan emerged on April 27, 1978. By that afternoon, the ground forces loyal to PDPA had seized the Ministry of Defense, the most important communication center for president loyalists, and Radio Afghanistan, which was the only national radio station at the time.

# Life Under
# Local Communism

A FEW EDUCATED AFGHANS, mainly from the big cities, supported the revolution and the political course of the new regime in Kabul, fearing the Islamic religious grip. However, the majority of poor and innocent Afghanis did not approve of the drastic change and obvious move toward communism. Soon after the coup, rural Afghan groups took up arms against the regime, which increasingly relied on Soviet arms for support.

Hit operations, bombings, military ambushes, secret kidnapping, and terrorism became a common part of the struggle against the communist regime, involving antigovernment forces as well as government police and military. Thousands of innocent people all around the country were imprisoned as a result of these activities.

Secret government and party operation started to become more intense due to increasing opposition, people's dissatisfaction, and the creation of various armed militias and groups within the country. Dictatorship and totalitarianism became the only visible signs of the regime's political attitude toward the public. No one could move around easily without fear of being watched, particularly the educated and government workers. This situation was particularly difficult for me because of my close ties to American embassy personnel, the Peace Corps, and the English language institute. I was in a very difficult and unsettling position, but I had to be very cautious and committed to our agreement at home to play it safe and not jeopardize my family and ultimate departure.

While chaos and organized resistance alike continued taking shape within all parts of the country, and the army imprisoned hundreds and thousands of men and women suspected of opposing the regime and communist party—and made mass disappearances and slaughter common practices—millions of Afghans started to seek refugee status, mainly in neighboring Pakistan and Iran. The few who could afford it made their way to India and Europe.

After taking a break from my good job at the Hotel Inter-Continental so that I could look after my family at home, I decided it was best for me to return to work, but the main question on everyone's mind was what would happen to the hotel management. The Hotel Inter-Continental's senior management consisted mainly of Americans and Europeans, so there was little doubt in everyone's mind about their replacement with local management. Our general manager and several foreign department heads remained fearful of losing their jobs.

Almost a week after the regime change, I was working on a banquet promotion when I was called to visit my boss. As I entered her office, she stood up, which was quite unusual. She put her arm around my shoulder and asked who I knew in this new government and regime. I was stunned and just looked at her with curiosity, since I had no idea to whom she was referring.

"You are to meet with the general manager; someone from the government has asked about you," she said. I honestly could not think of a single government employee or party person who would know me, except one of my cousins, who had been an established member of the Parcham party for a number of years.

My boss then walked me through the lobby and into the hotel's general manager's office.

"So, who are you and what do you know about this new government?" he asked.

I was once again completely puzzled and annoyed by what was taking place. "I honestly do not know anything. I am simply a worker here and have no connections with anyone in the new government," I stated.

He looked down with a frown as he sighed rather loudly. "Well, then, why are they asking for you at the government treasury department? Someone wants to see you," he said.

I told him once again that I had no idea what this call was all about, but said I would go to the treasury department to find out why they wanted to talk to me. I said, "I am honestly as curious as you are." He nodded as he stood up and told me to take the hotel car and go straight to the office of the Afghan Hotels Enterprise manager within the treasury department.

"Write down your name on this piece of paper and tell us who you are representing," a military officer shouted when I arrived. By this time, most government offices and authorities had been taken over and were guarded by military and police, so seeing armed guards and officials was no surprise, but finding a military officer within a civil service office was indeed a shock to me. I then realized that the new president of this agency must have come from the military ranks, too, which was becoming the norm.

The man behind the desk looked mean and imposing. He was dressed in a nice black suit and had a big mustache, which was a trademark of Khalq party members. I gave him my name as I moved toward his desk to shake hands as part of the customary introduction. He stood up and greeted me with a broad smile as he started speaking in Pashtu. "How are you? Do you remember Mr. Gulabzoi?" I honestly had no idea who Mr. Gulabzoi was and had indeed never heard of him before.

"No," I said.

"What do you mean?" he asked with a grimace.

I told him again that I honestly did not remember this name and asked him to help me by stating the man's first name.

"Said Mohammad Khan," he said.

The name still did not register, and I paused for a moment. I could then see the frustration in this officer's face as he shouted, "Said Mohammad Khan, of the air force!"

"Oh, oh, I remember him! Where is he?" I then remembered Said Mohammad Khan as the secretary of the air force's commanding officer during my military service, but I had known him only as Said Mohammad Khan, never as Gulabzoi.

Said Mohammad Khan was the man I had helped by safeguarding his books in my desk drawers and providing him with clean carbon copies of secret air force reports. I was happy to finally remember his name.

The manager then informed me that Said Mohammad had been shot and severely wounded during the coup d'etat and that he was resting in the hospital. "He has asked for your name and inquired if you were still working for the Inter-Continental," he continued.

As I left his office and went on my way to the hospital to see Said Mohammad, I recalled my service years and the friendship and support I had provided him as a soldier, doing favors for him without having any official association with his party. He was one of the officers I had taught English to as well, so he must have had fond memories of our relationship that had left a good impression on him.

As I entered his room, I looked anxiously toward the bed to see if I would indeed find the same gentleman I had worked with during my service years. He immediately turned his face toward me with a broad smile as he started to move his body upward to greet me. Not knowing the extent and nature of his injury, I tried to shake his hand while he removed the sheet from his body and extended his arm to try to hug me.

I quickly realized that he was wrapped heavily around the waist and chest area, and I told him not to move as we exchanged greetings. I asked him about the extent of his injury and what had really happened. He told me that he had spent a significant amount of time prior to the uprising at the air force base, right in the area of the office where we had served a few years back. He then told me that during the early-morning hours of the uprising, he had participated in a battle with members of the command-and-control brigade of the air force and had been struck by three bullets fired both from the ground and the air. A couple had penetrated his shoulder, but he had survived long enough to make it to the hospital.

I then asked what had made him think of me.

"I never thanked you enough for your support and courage during your service years," he said. "You did a lot and truly helped me accomplish my book distribution assignments. While sitting here, I was trying to remember the past and thought you might still be working at the Inter-Continental, so I inquired through various sources and instructed the man in charge of the Hotel Inter-Continental Kabul to find you."

I thanked him for remembering me and told him that I had actually been on my way to Iran on the day of the coup and that I was still happy but intended to further my education and experience outside of Afghanistan. He then started to tell me how proud and happy he was about the change and that he was now very satisfied, even if he had had to die to be part of the big change and the fact that people of Afghanistan were finally free and in charge of their own future.

He then asked about my role and what I would like to be at the hotel. "Why not the general manager?" he suggested.

I giggled a little as I started explaining the enormity of hotel management and the responsibilities that came along with it. I also informed him that managing the hotel through our Afghan organization and personnel would be impossible, as everything there was managed according to international standards and we simply didn't have the expertise and manpower to oversee the process.

"We shall see," he said, as he continued to smile and talk with a great sense of optimism and pride. I thanked him again for thinking of me and told him to visit as soon as he was out of the hospital.

"You used to tell us all about the hotel then, and now am I going to actually be able to see it?" he said.

I told him it would be great to welcome him there. Then he asked about my family, as he recalled my father's death during my service years. That was Said Mohammad Khan—always very gracious and thoughtful. He was truly a courageous, kind, and extremely sharp person with a great sense of honor and friendship, so visiting him at the hospital and reliving the thoughts and memories of military service were quite refreshing for me.

I went back to work the next day as usual, but still feeling the impact of my visit the day before with a key government official. I found myself isolated, while occasionally questioned by a few people inside my workplace. As a subsidiary of Afghan Hotels Enterprise, the Hotel Inter-Continental Kabul had been managed by Pan Am and Hotel Inter-Continental Corporation since its inception. While the majority of the Hotel Inter-Continental Kabul employees were Afghans, its key senior management consisted of American and European experts, so interaction with any communist government official or entity would be watched very closely. I decided to actively share the story of my visit with my friends and coworkers, as I did not want to them to see me as a communist party member or government agent. I wanted to be honest and simply share my military experience and the connection to Said Mohammad. It was a very strange and unsettling feeling, but I quickly learned that I was a target and a person to be feared no matter what I told them. In the meantime, we were slowly learning about certain other employees of the hotel, including several members of the security team, being potential party members and having ties to the government.

One member of the hotel's accounting office was actually seen as a leading party member and had the potential to secure a big promotion within the hotel ranks because of his affiliations. Meanwhile, we were also learning about the emergence of other leftist communist and nationalist groups within the hotel, so its fun, Western-style atmosphere was quickly changing into a more tense environment that was reminiscent of Soviet communism. Employees were no longer engaging; hotel managers were starting to simply look away and isolate themselves as much as possible. Our once friendly and cohesive workplace had suddenly changed to one of suspicion and fear.

Then news worsened. About three weeks after my visit with Mr. Alam Khan, my boss and I were called to the general manager's office again. We were informed to report to the treasury department along with a couple other midlevel managers from the hotel. I immediately thought about Alam Khan and his insistence that I seek higher positions within hotel management. While I could easily understand the rationale for my selection, I could not understand who would have recommended the other few who were supposed to report to the treasury, until I realized they must have been recommended by someone else with party or government ties.

Another two weeks passed, and then a bomb about several changes within hotel management was dropped. These changes were drafted and dictated by Afghan Hotels Enterprise, in conjunction with communist party members and hotel management. An accountant was promoted to assistant to the general manager, a former member of the food and beverage division was promoted to manager within his department—and I was promoted to manager of personnel.

I was completely devastated and honestly did not know how to handle the situation. While I had some confidence in my ability to assume enhanced responsibilities, the thought of managing a department of three hundred-plus employees was overwhelming and scary. After all, I had no prior experience in human resources/personnel management. But I did not dare say no, as refusing to not follow party and government direction would have brought about serious consequences.

However, because I had every intention of eventually leaving the country, I decided to simply manage my new responsibilities so as not to jeopardize my family and my future plans. As a matter of fact, I was more determined than ever to earn more money, learn more, and strengthen my connections with various agencies to provide security for my family and opportunities for our potential departure from Afghanistan and communist rule.

# The Russians Are Coming

THE HOTEL INTER-CONTINENTAL's occupancy rate had dropped to a low of 40 percent after all the political changes caused a huge drop in tourism in Afghanistan, but somehow the flow of foreign visitors to the hotel was getting back to normal toward the end of 1979—not because of tourists, but because the majority of residents happened to be foreign journalists and official government guests. We were all occupied with the usual activities, but there was an obvious change as a result of this influx, which included visits from very prominent figures from major media around the world, several of whom remained as hotel guests for longer periods.

Things would soon change even more, after an extreme leftist group abducted and ultimately assassinated American ambassador Adolph Dubs in February 1979. He was killed inside Kabul Hotel after the government refused to negotiate with his captors; with active participation from Soviet advisors, soldiers stormed his hotel room, which resulted in his death and the capture of his abductors. In the meantime, government and military secret-agent visits increased dramatically during October and November 1979, as tension was building and more and more people were being either imprisoned or murdered in mass killings, bombings, or open guerrilla warfare.

In order to help key members of hotel management in this time of need, when security concerns were widespread and the government had announced strict curfews, starting in the early evening, to limit the activities of Kabul residents, the Inter-Continental decided to provide complimentary rooms so that these employees could stay overnight. A few others and I were allowed to reside inside the hotel if we wanted to.

Meanwhile, furious fighting was visibly taking place all around the capital and countryside in general. The sound of nocturnal ground and air assaults was becoming routine; with high mountains separating Kabul's east and west and surrounding hills, the landscape turned into a fireworks spectacle, accompanied by patrolling tanks and helicopters. Some nights it was hard to sleep for more than a couple of hours. The people of Kabul welcomed the arrival of daylight, in hopes of not hearing gunfire and bombardments.

During the early-morning hours of December 27, 1979, when Kabul weather was close to negative temperatures and dark clouds hung all around, the city started to shake with the sound of planes flying overhead. It was a deep, grumbling noise that made it seem almost as if the entire city were experiencing a nonstop earthquake. The sound was heavy, unusual, and extremely difficult to identify. It forced thousands of residents to abandon crowded bazaars and congregations.

"What is this? This is not plane noise," shouted a coworker as we left our office and walked outside to see what was happening.

"I think they are military planes," I said.

"I know they sound like planes, but it is definitely more than planes," he said. "Can't you hear the entire ground shaking?" he yelled angrily. "Something big is happening!"

We looked up to see if we could pick out anything in the air, but the dark, thick clouds made it impossible. We understood why there were planes flying above, but why so low, so many, and so loud? The noise continued all day.

People retreated to their homes at 7:00 PM to honor the curfew, hoping for a calmer night and an end to the unbearable noise. But it was wishful thinking; the commotion continued throughout the evening and into the night. It felt as if the world was coming to an end.

The majority of hotel guests and journalists had hurriedly made their way back to the Inter-Continental when the noise began, but a few remained outside. The reporters' anxiety mounted as they awaited their friends' arrival inside the hotel lobby. Some ventured outside and onto the surrounding hills to hear the sound of flying planes and occasional gunfire. They had a perfect opportunity to look at the city below from the hotel windows, balconies, and pool. The cloud cover made it hard to see beyond a couple miles, so I was faced with the decision of venturing home or staying in the hotel. I procrastinated for a few hours, unsure of what to do.

After eating dinner and playing a round of ping-pong, we were approached by a hotel security guard, who warned us about extreme conditions outside and the fact that an all-out war was breaking. We ran toward the pool area to see what was happening, and there it was—the city looked just like a war zone. We could hear gunfire and see spectacular explosions and fires around the hills and outskirts of the city. The area closer to Kabul's only airport, adjacent to the military airport, seemed to be a big target. Not just chaos, but uncertainty about the culprits involved in this latest move, was palpable among all of us as we looked and listened in awe, feeling helpless and betrayed.

"My God, what is happening to us?" screamed one of the hotel workers, with tears in his eyes, while he covered his face with his hands. "What will happen to my children?" he sighed.

Within half an hour, the hotel issued instructions to turn off the lights and for everyone to go inside their rooms and not stand in any outside areas or balconies; hotel guards started guiding guests and employees to safe locations.

"I have to go to home," I yelled to my friends and coworkers.

"You are crazy, Atta!" shouted an elderly worker. "We have no idea who is in control—this is no joke! This is different!"

I returned to my room to put on comfortable clothes and leave, even though I knew it was going to be a very long and dangerous walk. I changed in a matter of minutes and walked to the back door of the hotel, where I was confronted by Amir Gul, a longtime hotel security guard.

"Please do not go out!" he yelled in Pashtu.

"I must go home, but I promise I will be careful and go through back roads," I assured him.

He just stood there looking at me, visible tears in his eyes. I knew he was quite upset, but he did not say anything more; he reached out to open the back door leading to the garden area and onto the hill below. By then it was pitch dark, and the sound of gunfire was constant and could be heard all across the city.

Once outside, I contemplated which way to go, then started climbing the hill to the north of the hotel in hopes of going down the hill rather than walking through the bushes and heavy shrubs and trees of Bagh-e Bala, a historic garden. I quickly noticed that the big Qargha military base looked like a giant fireball as a result of constant shelling. Looking toward the center of Kabul city, I could see heavy gunfire and bombardments of the main government and military bases, so I knew it was either a big military uprising or an imminent invasion by Russia. I then realized that going down the hill was not a good idea, so I turned back and decided to move slowly between trees and make my way down the big hillside to the main road. Although I had no intention of walking on that road, I wanted be as close as possible to avoid being noticed by residents.

As I descended about half a mile and got close to the main road, I started to see military armored cars advancing toward Qargha, too close to the road, so I turned and decided to go down toward Karte Parwan through vineyards, which would be more secure than the main pathways. I stumbled and fell many times in the dark, but quickly realized that I was not the only one in the area; I started to notice movement in the vineyards. I immediately sat under a tree for about twenty minutes to find out if these people in the area were ordinary people or government or military personnel. I listened carefully as I saw three groups of people making their way down the hill. I heard a baby crying and his father start yelling at him, and I realized these people were also trapped in the area, and that there was no reason to fear anyone.

As I stood up, two men starting advancing toward me. "What are you doing here?" they asked.

"I am going home," I said.

"We are going home, too; we just wanted to make sure you are not one of them," they replied.

I told them I was simply on my way home and had no idea what was happening. *"Ba khair bureie,"* they said. "Be safe."

"You, too," I yelled.

As I continued for another half mile, I had to duck as the ground shook from a huge explosion on the mountainside to the right. As I looked up, I saw a fireball close to the main television tower on the mountaintop, and started to see serious shelling of the military base closest to our home area. I was by then completely determined to continue and make it home, so I started walking faster, out of the vineyards and into residential areas, hiding behind homes and alleys when military cars passed. Finally, I made it Naderia High School, where I then had to choose between continuing on the main road leading to the city and taking smaller, surrounding streets.

As I was about to run across the main highway, I realized tanks were approaching the area on that road, so I quickly jumped over the wall and into the schoolyard. I was literally only a few feet away from my old art classroom when bullets started flying all around the schoolyard. I realized that I had been noticed, so I ducked down and lay beneath the big building concrete wall for almost half an hour, but when I heard footsteps right behind the schoolyard, I decided to run and hide under the stairs leading to the building. Looking out through the stairs, I could see flashes of passing military cars' lights, followed by tanks. I kept waiting for someone to start looking for me, but they kept on marching.

This caravan was long; it took a good thirty minutes before the area was cleared. I then retreated to the south side of the building and climbed through the wall and onto the street leading toward home. I knew I had to take advantage of the time I had, and started running hard. In a matter of minutes, I was in a narrow alley very close to my friend Sami's house; then I heard the sound of approaching tanks again along the main highway. I realized staying in the alley was not a smart move, and decided that I should knock on a door—but what if no one opened it quickly enough? I knew I would be out in the open and visible to approaching tanks. This was a rather quiet area of Karte Parwan, and I could not find a single soul on the street at the time. As I kept on walking, in one house I heard the sound of two people whispering to each other as the call came: "You better get out of the area, or I will shoot you." I immediately started running, ducking at times to avoid hitting trees but also to avoid being noticed.

Fortunately, I remembered another very narrow alley on the west side of the road leading to the main road that was closer to Sami's house. I started running toward the end of the alley, hugging a wall as I went. When I reached the end of this long alley, I lay low and scanned the main road. Sami's home was only about five hundred yards away, but on the other side of the road, so I had no choice but to cross the road once I was ready. I could not stand in front of the door and knock, so my only thought was to jump over the wall that enclosed Sami's house.

I then started to hear the arrival of more tanks and military cars, so I lay flat on the ground while occasionally looking from side to side to see the length and passage of these cars. Finally, the moment came when I felt safe enough to reach Sami's house, and I got on my feet and started to run.

I ran fast for almost about twenty yards. When I heard the sound of more cars and shots being fired in my direction, I stumbled for a moment, but then started running again and jumped over the wall leading to Sami's home. Fortunately, the shots were being fired for the sole purpose of scaring people and enforcing the strict curfew, for it would have very easy for the soldiers to chase me and get into Sami's home if they wanted to.

Once I was behind the wall and inside the yard area, I moved toward the entrance of the house, but I did not want to scare anyone, so I retreated and started knocking on the main door. Sami's younger brother immediately appeared from the second door and started walking through the small alley from the house toward the main entrance door with a flashlight in his hand.

"Who is it?" he yelled.

"Attaullah," I whispered loudly enough so he could hear.

He stood there in shock. I again told him it was me, and that I had just jumped over the wall as I was being chased by military.

He ran toward me and gave me a big hug as he said, *"Shukor khuda ya."* ("Thank God you are okay"). He led me only a few yards away into a small guest room that Sami and his brothers had built for gatherings. Funnily enough, they had named this room the Inter-Continental. "Let's go to the Inter-Continental, and I will call Sami and let the family know you are here," Sami's brother said.

"Are you crazy?" Sami yelled, pulling me into his arms, when he appeared. I told him what had happened that day, but said I still planned to make it home that night. He was visibly shaken, and not happy with my decision. His family were some of the kindest people on Earth; they immediately prepared food and tea as we listened to the radio. By then Sami and his family had fully figured out that the uprising was the work of hardcore communists and meant a potential full-scale invasion by Russia, because of the enormity of military traffic and the intensity of the events during the day and early-evening hours.

After a couple hours' wait, things got calmer, and I decided to make my way home. I was then only about two miles away from home, but faced the very difficult task of making it across the main road leading to Shahrara, which was the main entry to the second military depot and central reserve force of the city. The only other option was to walk past the Salang Highway. Despite the extremely cold weather, I left Sami's home and ran, hiding behind homes and alleys, across the main highway and into the fruit market area. The only way to cross the fruit market was to walk through alleys, which would normally be guarded by night patrolmen.

I waited for a good twenty minutes at the entrance of the market to see any patrol movement but could not see anyone. I was quite confident then that the guards and patrol had given up and were somehow running for their lives, too, so I started to slowly make my way along the walls in order to avoid being seen. It was completely silent, with very few lights on within each aisle. Many shopkeepers and workers who slept in their shops must have left for home, not wanting to risk their lives by spending the night inside their stores— it must not have seemed worth it that night. I began to feel more comfortable and slowed to a jog, not running fast enough to scare anyone or be mistaken for a thief.

I finally made it home safely and started knocking on our door. "Is everyone home?" I asked my brother Zia as he opened it.

"Yes," he responded. What a feeling! It was an incredibly gratifying and happy moment as we embraced. "Why did you not stay at the hotel?" he asked.

I told him I had been worried about the family and had simply felt it was a good idea to be home; plus, I was worried about the huge military base and ammunition depot close to our house. Located in the hills behind our home, it had been pounded heavily, and we could still see and hear powerful explosions, gunfire, and the movement of tanks all around the city, as planes continued to fly above us throughout the night.

"What are they flying?" I asked. "Planes don't sound like that."

"They are carrying tanks," Zia answered. "That is the sound and noise of big transport planes carrying tanks. Those are damn

Russian planes," he said, as if he knew exactly what was happening and Russians were indeed invading.

Zia was extremely upset and kept pacing. My mother got mad at us because we kept going out to the main street to look for potential military activity within the neighborhood. We spent the night talking and drinking tea, as there was no chance of sleeping. It felt like the whole ground was moving as a result of the ongoing activity; fear and uncertainty overwhelmed everyone, particularly the girls, who were young and scared, and to whom it was very difficult to explain what was happening.

Zia got mad at the girls and challenged them to be brave. But how could we expect that of them when we could clearly hear gunfire even from inside our rooms? He and I decided to climb up on top of the house to see which areas were being bombarded. The most notable target under fire was the presidential palace and surrounding area, but it was clear that many other sites and military installations around the city were being attacked as well. Surrounded by mountains and hills, Kabul was burning like a bowl of fire.

As snow started to fall, it made for a perfect climate for Russian invasion. We wondered if Kabul had ever in history witnessed such a moment of despair, sorrow, and uncertainty. It felt and sounded like the stories of Russian invasion of Poland and Czechoslovakia. It was one thing to learn about a country's invasion through history books and local news, but it felt surreal and daunting to experience firsthand the invasion of your motherland by a superpower. While we all felt betrayed and frustrated, we also felt that the invaders would not last in our homeland and it would simply be a matter of time before they left. For now, we just wanted the night to be over so that we could get out of our homes and start our fight for the freedom of our beloved country.

# The Red Dawn

AFTER MANY EXCRUCIATING HOURS of sleepless waiting, it was time to face the harsh reality of a red dawn and being invaded by the Russian army. Zia and I left our home and walked to the main road, where we noticed our usual group of friends gathered. It was still rather dark; people were contemplative and sharing their thoughts.

"They are on the other side of the market!" a young boy yelled, as he emerged running uphill from the fruit market. "The Russians are here, I swear they are here, with their tanks and machine guns... Be careful—they just shot at a runaway car!"

Over a hundred young men started running toward the fruit market alley to see for themselves.

We were confronted by a rumbling Soviet armored column, but there was only shock, not fear, in people's eyes. Russians on the tanks were trying to hand out biscuits, chocolates, and chewing gum to children, but no one would take them. Other Russian tanks had taken position at key traffic circles, and Russian soldiers, as well as a few Afghan military personnel and Afghan communist members, identified by red or white armbands, were at their side, directing traffic.

We were not afraid, just extremely cautious, as we tried to ascertain if this was indeed a reality. In a matter of moments, we were at the other end of the fruit market, adjacent to the main paved road, where dozens of tanks and armored personnel were crossing. And there they were—yes, it was the Russians! For an instant I thought we were watching another Russian war movie, and I immediately thought of the Russian invasion of Czechoslovakia and Poland. I had read and heard about the invasion of Eastern European countries, but it was hard to believe it was Afghanistan's turn. As we stood there, I could see tears flowing down the cheeks of quite a few of us from the neighborhood as we looked on in a state of complete shock.

We could still hear the sound of gunfire and artillery in remote areas, and we were told that the nearest military depot, less than two miles away, had not surrendered and was surrounded by Russian troops. At that point we noticed at least twenty tanks headed toward this military base, again bringing up vivid memories of war movies we had seen during last few years. It truly felt unreal.

Humiliated and extremely frustrated, we immediately began thinking and talking about fighting back against the Russian invaders. The people of Afghanistan had had a difficult time accepting the notion of going the communist route since the moment our own local communist regime had taken over, let alone the invasion of our proud and innocent Muslim nation by communist Russia!

After watching this parade of invading troops on our own soil, we knew it was time to go home and break the news to the family. But when Zia and I entered our house, we found our mother and sisters sobbing; we did not have to explain anything—they had already found out. My two brothers and I gathered to discuss our responsibility to safeguard our family, but ultimately we decided to go to work and strategize our next moves later. I changed my clothes and prepared to depart, while instructing everyone else not to leave the house.

My younger brother, Zia, had already joined one of the main antigovernment groups months prior to the Russian invasion, but we had not shared this news openly with the female members of our family. We were therefore very concerned about his exposure, but he convinced us that he would be more careful and assured us about his determination and further motivation to defend our motherland. He promised to fight secretly and not jeopardize the family or anyone's life, but it was now time to get out and face the fact of our occupation by an invading Russia.

I left the house and started to walk toward Karte Parwan, but I was told the road ahead was closed due to the military siege, so I had to walk through the fruit market and onto the main paved road. I continued to walk for about two miles to the main intersection, where I saw the Russian presence firsthand. The whole intersection area was occupied with Russian troops, tanks, and artillery, which were stopping cars and allowing them to move after a quick check. Along with a handful of other Afghans, I crossed the intersection and hailed a cab. "To Hotel Inter-Continental," I told him.

He looked at me and said, "Do you think the hotel is still there?"

I told that I had been there the previous evening, and that unless something had happened later in the night, the hotel would still be standing. He said he lived in the area and had noticed lots of shelling behind the hotel, mentioning that the target may have been the Qargha Urdu garrison, which stood only a few miles away from the Inter-Continental.

At that point, there were not too many cars on Kabul streets, so it was an easy and quick ride. As we reached the hotel area, I did not witness a single guard by the entrance, which was shocking until I realized that no uniformed personnel would wish to be visible at the moment.

"The hotel is intact!" yelled a hotel security guard as we approached the entrance. Shah Mahmood, a longtime security guard and captain of the hotel's national dance team, was a big, handsome man with a full mustache. He looked distressed and agitated as he held the door open for me. While there was no one besides him outside the hotel, the inside was buzzing with foreign journalists ready to explore the day after the Russian invasion. They were moving equipment and sitting throughout the lobby, waiting anxiously for further instructions about whether they could go outside the area. Within a couple hours, after realizing no government or military personnel had come around the hotel area, many of the journalists ventured out and scattered all over the city.

As the day passed, spotty resistance from military posts gave way to ultimate surrender to Russian troops all around the country, and then it was official: Afghanistan had been invaded by almost one hundred thousand Russian soldiers—working in conjunction with the local Parcham communist party—over a forty-eight-hour time span. The whole country was now under the control of Russian forces and remaining loyal members of the Afghan communist military. Hundreds of top-level opposing party members and military and government officials were executed, and thousands were thrown in prison.

Quite a few members of the Khalq communist party joined forces with resistance groups around the country, but because the people of Afghanistan had already seen widespread mobilization of armed guerillas, there was no sign of an immediate reaction in the form of open demonstrations by masses. It was becoming clear that armed resistance would be the way to defend the motherland, rather than jeopardizing families and innocent people by taking to the streets of the capital.

Within a few weeks, life in Kabul appeared to have slipped back almost to normal. We saw Russians in the bazaars; they were the shopkeepers' best customers. But they were not aggressive in public. The biggest change was that there was suddenly vodka for sale everywhere. Shop windows were full of Russian caps and uniforms, which soldiers had sold to get money to buy vodka, hashish, and Afghan curios.

In daytime, the Soviet forces and Afghan allies ruled most of the roads and major intersections. But as darkness fell and the curfew took over, all traffic would stop and the resistance forces would start their operation. They had a sense of every area's weak spots and always struck when we least expected. Using ambushes, land mines, and even knives if they could get close enough, they had become masters of hit-and run attacks. They knew the Soviet retaliation was swift and deadly, so they killed and then fled for their lives.

Russian forces started to experience huge casualties as mujahideen fighters put fear in their eyes. There were tales of Soviet prisoners being skinned alive or having their eyes gouged out with bayonets upon capture. When it came to fighting, many of the mujahideen proved to be fearless warriors.

# Well Full of Weapons

ZIA HAD STARTED TO SECRETLY safeguard ammunition and weapons and deliver them to various locations within his designated area of responsibility. We decided to keep it a secret for a while, as we knew our older brother and mother would not allow us to put our entire family at risk. Zia was able to stash small amounts of ammunition without any problem, but within a few months we realized it was becoming more and more dangerous, as a result of increased patrolling and searches for weapons throughout Kabul. My brother and his friends had to minimize their activities by delivering larger amounts of weapons, in order to avoid multiple trips out of our neighborhood. However, Zia did warn me that he would soon be delivering twenty-five to fifty units of high-priced machine guns and handguns for distribution to members of the resistance surrounding the Kabul airport.

I arrived home after work one day to find Zia and his friends, young men who were determined to join the resistance forces, congregating outside our house. This was a familiar group, as the majority of them were members of our soccer club, so I felt very comfortable talking to them. They had innocently thought it was okay for them to gather as they had in the past, not realizing they would no longer be safe out in the open, so I quickly suggested they go inside our home yard.

After the group dispersed, Zia told me about the scheduled delivery of several pieces of ammunition that evening, to be stored at our house and a few other locations in the area. I was informed that the weapons would arrive in a taxi pretending to drop off passengers with luggage. We would wait until night fell and it was safer before carrying the weapons into the house.

When the five big, full bags of ammunition arrived, we hurried inside the house and hid them right away, deep under a stairway where wood for home heating purposes was stored. My brother informed me that similar weapon delivery would be taking place throughout the week, all over the city, as resistance groups planned to launch their fight within a few days.

A few days later, I arrived home early to find the entire neighborhood surrounded by tanks and armed military personnel.

"What is going on?" I asked a long-bearded shopkeeper, Sofi, whose store was close to the alley leading to my home.

"The neighborhood is being searched for weapons," he replied. "Your brother Zia was looking for you," he continued.

I rushed inside the house to find Zia very upset and anxious. "We need to move the weapons right away," he said. I asked him where our older brother, Qudrat, was. He said Qudrat and his friends had been informed about the situation and were on their way home.

"Have they started the search?" I asked Zia. He told me that all of Shahrara was being surrounded, and that the search had already started on the south side of the neighborhood. He said the prominent leaders of the area were very unhappy and were attempting to block or delay the search of homes, as they saw the action as an insult. He also mentioned that several leaders were out there negotiating with military and secret-service personnel, and said he had already asked for help, since he knew our father and our family were widely respected locally. In the meantime, we were quite happy that the search had started away from our home and that we would most probably not be not looked at that day, as it was getting late. But then we learned that searches had continued throughout the night in other neighborhoods, so we could only hope to avoid or at least delay the search so we could get the weapons out of the area.

When our older brother and his longtime friend Sakhi arrived home, we immediately started to strategize about how to secure the hidden weapons in a safer area, but we knew we had no way of transporting them away from our home. The obvious choice was to either dig a hole in the yard or dump them in a sewer.

"The best option is the well," mentioned Sakhi.

"But it is quite deep," my brother told him—there was no way we could lower them all down there, besides the fact that the water might not be deep enough to hold twenty-plus machine guns.

"Well, the French units are quite small, but the Russian Kalashnikovs may be a problem."

"Who wants to go down this deep well?" asked my older brother.

"I am the smallest amongst the group so I volunteer," Sakhi said. He was a very well-educated man and had an excellent job as a computer programmer at IBM at the time, but we knew he was a devoted friend to our family and would do anything to help.

"You're the man, but let's go check it first," Zia replied.

Sakhi was only five-foot-four and weighed about 120 pounds, so he seemed to be the logical choice among the four of us.

We then informed our mother and sisters, who had been looking out from inside the rooms in fear and total silence as we stood and talked only a few feet away from the well about our plans. My mother knew she had no choice but to inform the girls about the weapons stored inside the house. We all knew they would now be extremely scared, and we even considered getting all the women out of the house, but we decided that would only send a bad signal and attract further suspicion.

"I will go talk to the elders and hope to delay the search," Qudrat said, as he instructed us to start the process. My mother had cut at least five big blankets into pieces in order to help. We wrapped Sakhi securely with multiple long pieces of cloth, along with doubled-up rubber rope around his waist and an additional long rope as an extra cautionary measure.

With evening closing in, it was now time to wrap up the weapons, so my mother and sisters started searching for all the plastic bags they could find in the house. But there were not enough, so a couple of us went out to find as much plastic as we could. When we realized we still did not have enough to cover all the weapons, my brother Zia instructed us to wrap them in clothing—there was no time to contemplate.

After securing the house entrance, one of our group went up on the roof, and then it was time for Sakhi to descend into the well. We lowered him carefully the first time, along with two Kalashnikovs, as he made good use of footholds that the well diggers had made. Without his flashlight, he would have been completely invisible inside the hole.

"Great news!" he shouted loudly, from deep inside the well. "We have about two to three feet of water here."

We then started to lower the rest of the weapons by putting three to four units inside fifty-pound flour sacks. We had instructed Sakhi to make sure he spread out the units under the water to avoid any suspicious movement; Zia had mentioned that the search groups, particularly Russians, would be using flashlights all over to spot hidden locations. It took Sakhi a good fifteen minutes to complete this dangerous task and climb up.

When we pulled him out of the well, we realized he had completely run out of oxygen and was having trouble catching his breath as he sat on the floor. Zia kept on looking down into the well with the flashlight to ensure nothing was visible inside.

"I can see plastic there!" yelled Zia.

"Oh my God," I shouted, as we ran toward the well to look down. Sure enough, a piece of plastic was visibly floating on top of the water.

"Sorry, friend, but you have to go back in," my older brother told Sakhi.

"I will have to catch my breath," he mentioned with a smile. We were extremely grateful to him as we lowered him back into the well to push down or tie up the plastic.

"Stay there for a while to make sure it is okay," my brother told him.

"All good," Sakhi said with confidence as he started climbing back up again.

Still, we kept looking down the well for a good half hour just to make sure everything looked okay. Those few hours were without the doubt the most dangerous and agonizing moments of our entire lives, as capture of these weapons would mean the end of us. We spent the next couple hours just talking with our mother and sisters and preparing them to answer questions appropriately.

We knew that almost all of these searches included questioning of all adults and even young children.

Around nine thirty that night came the word that security forces were closing in on our home and would be coming for a search within ten minutes, but that the elders of Shahrara had lobbied hard on our behalf, convincing many of the Afghan officers to take it easy and respect the privacy of families, particularly women and young children. When another hour or so had passed, still no one had come to search our home or the homes of our immediate neighbors.

"They are pulling their units out of the neighborhood!" called our neighbor as he rushed through the alley toward us. "They are no longer searching!"

I run inside the house to inform my mother and sisters, who had gathered to read the Quran and pray.

"We are going to be okay! They are leaving, so there is nothing to worry about," I told them. My mother embraced me and ordered us to take all weapons out of the well and house right away. I assured her that we would do so. We then all celebrated in silence and enjoyed a dinner together, but informed Sakhi and my brothers that we still had work to do. I told Zia to make arrangements and get the weapons out before the military showed up again, but he assured me orders had been already issued to transport them out of the area before noon the next day.

Shortly after dinner, we were back at it, lowering Sakhi down inside the well to dig out the weapons—which at first seemed like an easy task, until we all realized that it was extremely difficult for him to tie and secure the weapons while in water in pitch darkness. We decided to make use of flour bags again, but managed to pull up only two units at a time. It was a good two hours before we were able to get all of the weapons out of the well, dry them, and pack them inside suitcases for delivery as luggage.

In order to act as if nothing out of the ordinary had occurred, we all decided to go about our usual business the next day, relying on our mother to help guide the arriving antigovernment fighters and hand them the suitcases. We were informed before midnight, however, that the delivery would actually take place right after morning prayers and sunrise. Sakhi, my older brother, and I spent the entire night in our guesthouse, located on the second floor right above our home entryway, just to make sure we would be ready to react in case something went wrong. It was impossible to sleep that night.

Finally, Zia announced, "They are here!" But then he said the driver would take only three suitcases and the remaining ones would be taken within the half hour. They had made arrangements for two cabs to deliver the cases, to avoid any suspicion. We brought out the three cases and loaded them inside the car, which took off as soon as the cases were in. Then came some tense moments, as the second car did not show up almost for a full hour.

"Okay, let's move very quickly!" yelled Zia, as we hurried to move the remaining two cases into the second cab, which was backed into the alley to avoid being noticed by the main street's traffic. Within seconds, the car took off, and we finally felt like the real danger had dissipated. As we went back inside the house, my mother faced us right at the entrance and warned us to no longer endanger the lives of our family. We assured her this would never happen again, and that we knew it was time to start planning in earnest to take the entire family out of the country.

# Forced to Flee

IN THE WEEKS FOLLOWING the incident with the well, my brothers and I began formulating plans to leave the country. I was taken into custody and interrogated three times, so my family insisted I be the first to find a way to leave and said they would follow after my departure.

I thought it was time to make best of my connections and look at the possibility of obtaining a passport to leave the country. About seven months had passed since the big Russian invasion, and I was clearly in danger, so it was time to leave Afghanistan before it was too late. I had the choice of fleeing to a neighboring country or getting an official passport. The government did not issue any tourist passports at the time, and only the elite and wealthy could find a way to obtain one. I thought about seeking help from an old and powerful friend—Said Mohammad Khan, my military officer—since he was a big shot within the cabinet and could easily issue his approval of my passport.

Realizing that the communist government did not wish to see many people leave the country and so had severely limited issuance of passports, I reluctantly made the decision to go and talk to him directly and inform him of my decision to leave the country to pursue higher education. I was admitted to his office without much delay. We exchanged greetings, and he asked about the hotel and how everything was going. I right away reminded him about my desire to travel abroad to further my education and improve my professional career, which I had shared with him during my military service year.

"I remember very well," he said, and asked where I would like to go. I told him that I wished to join one of the Middle Eastern or Southeast Asian Inter-Continental hotels.

Alam Khan was an extremely smart man and told me with a smile to write my request for a passport. I happily prepared my request the next day and obtained his approval on the spot. As I thanked him, he gave me a big hug and handshake and said, "Be very careful." I knew he cared a lot about me and wanted me to play it very safe.

I was very appreciative of his gesture and thoughts about me, and grateful for his advice and support. That moment was one of the most memorable and happiest in my life; I realized I had the ability to help my family now. But I knew I had a very tough road ahead in terms of keeping my departure plans completely secret. My family's decision was to not share the news with anyone but my mother and two brothers. Not that we did not trust my sisters, but they were all too young, and the risk of sharing any part of my plan have would been too grave.

I then went to work on obtaining a visa in order to purchase an airline ticket. That was another big hurdle, and it had to be carried out in secret, as I was well known to many agents and workers of Ariana Afghan Airlines because of my long-term work relationship with them as a representative of the Hotel Inter-Continental.

With help from a friend, I was able to obtain a short-term visa from Austria's embassy in Kabul, and I booked a flight to Austria, with a stop in Germany, at the earliest convenience. I knew my next capture would be the end for the entire family, and realized that my brother Zia's active fight against Russia was not going to go unnoticed, despite all his careful planning.

My original idea was to find a way to remain in Germany, where quite a few friends of mine had been accepted for political asylum; but I realized there was no guarantee, so I tried to pick at least one more destination as an option. Despite having a valid passport and visa to Austria, I had a real fear of being stopped at Kabul airport, as I was familiar to so many school and work associates. After I shared my concern with one of my brother's closest friends, he told me to find a way to make some changes to the original passport that I had obtained, so we were able to alter the birth date and photo to make the document look a little different. I also started to grow a mustache.

Only a few days before I was scheduled to leave, I still had not told every member of my family. What a horrible feeling.

"I am sorry, but I am leaving for Austria this week," I finally told my sisters, with tears running from my eyes. They were completely stunned at first, but then everyone started crying for joy at the knowledge that one of us was going to get out. They also knew that this move was going to open the door for the rest of the family. We spent the entire night talking and hugging and crying as though we were never going to see each other again.

My mother was visibly worried and was getting sicker and sicker by the minute as my departure approached. I had to leave the house alone in order to not draw attention to my plan. My brother had delivered my only carry-on bag to the airport earlier. Then it was time to say goodbye. My heart started pounding, and tears kept streaming down my eyes and face. I realized it was actually time to motivate the girls and my mother, but knew it could be my last goodbye, so I felt as if there was no tomorrow or chance of seeing them again. I was filled with anxiety and frustration, but a little hope at the same time.

We drove away from my neighborhood and onto the main highway toward the airport, and I could not hold back my tears as I continued to look at everything outside for the last time—my entire family, our people, our land, our hopes, and the questions surrounding the future of my beloved country! It was a somber day.

Our plan was to not arrive too early at the airport, but to try to get there at the last minute in order to avoid further exposure. As we got out of the taxi, my brother carried my carry-on baggage so that I could pretend to be just visiting the airport. Not a whole lot of activity was happening around the airport, except for a crowd of well-wishers and a few who were preparing to leave. We timed it well enough to get there only half an hour before my flight, so as soon as we were inside the airport building I grabbed the baggage from my brother without hugging or shaking hands, shouted, *"Khuda hafez"* ("May Allah be with you"), and walked straight toward customs with my head down, trying to hide my face from onlookers. We had worked with a friend to get my passport checked, instead of taking the risk of being checked by any agent, since the original passport was slightly altered.

I waited for a few minutes and leaned on a big pole to avoid full exposure in the crowded area until my name was called. This was not the normal procedure, so we made it sound like I had been checked already and somehow was waiting for clearance. When my name was called, I was quickly led through the hallway and toward the plane. The person helping me was supposed to walk through the hallway until I was out of the main building, at which time I had to walk about a couple hundred feet to the plane.

Completely shaken, I started walking toward the plane, still keeping my head down and trying to stay inside the group to avoid being noticed from the airport area. I was very conscious of the tight security and the watchful eyes of secret agents in the area, so every step closer I got to the plane was a big accomplishment, but there truly was no sense of safety, even as I finally started climbing the stairs and onto the plane.

I was greeted and led to my window seat in the fifth row on the left side of the plane. I wanted to sit so badly, and felt as if I had walked miles, as exhaustion penetrated me. I was still hesitant to look up outside the plane, for some reason, despite being inside and feeling halfway safe and on the way to leaving my beloved country. I wanted badly to cry out loud, but tried to keep my composure as the other passengers boarded. I finally thought it was time to look around a little, but when I glanced outside I saw a dozen armed soldiers walking toward the plane, holding their Kalashnikovs upward.

*Oh, great*, I told myself. They were coming to get me! I knew there was too much risk involved in flying out of Kabul, in light of my image and the developments of the last few months. As I watched, I saw the soldiers lining up in two rows in front of the plane stairway; everything came to a halt, and people continued to look outside and try to figure out what was going to happen.

Everyone was quite fearful, whispering throughout the plane. Since Afghanistan's takeover by communist forces, people overall had become very quiet and accustomed to not questioning a whole lot, in fear of retaliation and the feeling of being surrounded by a government or party agent.

After about half an hour of this anxiety, someone mentioned, "We will be accompanied by a big government official. Let's see who it might be."

That statement made me a little more comfortable, but there was still no time to celebrate. By then every passenger's eyes were glued to the windows and the airport building as tension mounted. A group of six or seven people then emerged from the side of the airport building and moved toward the plane, but it was still hard to see who they were. As they got closer, I quickly recognized Abdul Wakil, our secretary of finance, and I was quite shaken, as he knew me very well after his recent meeting with all the key personnel of the Hotel Inter-Continental. I was sure this was the moment when I would be captured and not allowed to fly.

I am not sure what I was thinking, as he was never going to sit in the back with the rest of the passengers, but the idea of first class and VIP seating never crossed my mind at that moment. As he was led to the plane, I simply kept my head down for fear of being recognized. But when the plane was finally ready for departure, I started to feel more comfortable again. As the plane took off and flew over the city of my birth, I could no longer hold back the flow of tears.

"Why are you crying, young man?" asked a gentleman in his sixties sitting next to me. "What is the matter?"

I told him that I had a sick family member whom I had left behind and said I was feeling bad; I could not tell him that I was leaving the country for good. He started to comfort me and told me he was a businessman and he, too, no longer enjoyed traveling abroad, for fear of leaving his family in harm's way.

"How long does it take to leave Afghanistan?" I asked him.

He smiled and said, "What do you mean?"

I told him, "Leaving the Afghan land."

"Oh, it is about two hours."

I then began looking down at everything I could spot. At first it was hard to see much besides mountains and miles of desert, but I continued to watch for as long as I could, crying constantly. I was also too embarrassed to look around, as I would make my departure and reasons too obvious, but fortunately, the older man went to sleep right after takeoff, and the younger boy in the aisle seat did not care what was going on around him. I did not stop crying for even a moment until the pilot announced we had left Afghan land and were entering Iran territory. That was when I finally realized that this plan would not backfire, and that I would ultimately make my way to Europe.

As a child, I had heard the word "refugee" and learned what it meant in reference to Jews, Palestinians, Romanians, etc.; I even knew Afghanistan had had its own refugees from other countries throughout history, including over fifty Jewish families who had migrated to Afghanistan and lived inside our capital.

The thought of having refugees in my own country was one thing, but the idea of being forced out of my homeland and seeking refuge elsewhere was another thing entirely, and was the scariest thought of all.

# Where to Go?

I HAD NO IDEA WHERE I would end up. All I was thinking about after leaving my homeland was how to secure a home outside of Afghanistan. Thousands of refugees were settling in other European countries, but Germany seemed like a safer bid because I had many friends there and it was becoming a second home for several of my former soccer club members, including three Afghan national team players. As a matter of fact, the Afghan national team's political asylum in Germany had made international news a few months prior, and had opened the door for acceptance of Afghan refugees into other European countries. In case I was not allowed to stay in Germany, I had heard that people had a better chance of making it to the United States, Canada, or England from Austria, so that seemed like a logical backup destination.

"What a weird feeling," I said when my plane landed in Germany, without any regard for who was listening. I was not anxious to get off the plane quickly, and was happy to be almost the last passenger to walk out.

Because hundreds of thousands of illegal immigrants were arriving to European nations, and particularly to Germany, there was a visible presence of armed German police and customs agents. I waited for a good forty-five minutes before I approached the customs officer. I extended my passport and immediately informed him that I was here to stay as a political refugee. He frowned at me while examining me thoroughly and looking carefully at my passport. I had not seen myself in the mirror, but realized I must look terrible, as I had been crying for the duration of the flight from Kabul to Frankfurt. I was asked to move over to the desk of a middle-aged officer and then to a waiting area, where I sat motionless for a good half hour, until a uniformed officer came through a revolving door and starting walking toward me with my passport in his hand.

"Come with me," he said, as he pulled me by my arm into an office. I sat in a chair at a desk in this small room, which seemed to be designed for interrogations. I was there for about another half hour as I anxiously awaited questioning; finally, two armed officers entered the room, followed by women in uniform.

"Sprechen sie Deutsch?" one officer asked. I knew they were referring to German, but I responded in English and told him no, I spoke only English, Farsi, and Pashto. The officer looked up and gestured to the woman standing by the door. I was nervous, reminded of Nazi interrogations during World War II.

"What do you want?" was her first question.

"I am asking for asylum. I just came from Afghanistan," I told them.

"Are you alone?" she asked.

"Yes," I responded, and told her I had a big family but had left them all behind, as my life was in danger.

"Where did you learn English? You speak it very well."

I told her I had learned it years ago and had worked for the United States Information Services' library and the Hotel Inter-Continental for a number of years. The officers seemed to lighten up a little.

"When did you work for them?" the woman asked.

"I was working there until I left Afghanistan."

"Who do you know here in Germany?"

I could think of many friends in Germany who had arrived during the last several months but thought mentioning my former soccer teammates would probably be most helpful, so I told them about the three players I knew who were members of the Afghan national team.

"Do you know anyone here in Frankfurt?" one of the male officers asked.

I told him about my very good friend Homayoun, a former colleague at the Hotel Inter-Continental.

They started talking in German to each other, while the first officer left the room temporarily. He returned in about ten minutes. During this time the woman continued to ask unofficial questions about my family and the conditions in Afghanistan. She told me how exhausted I looked and that my eyes were completely red. I was very hungry and thirsty and had a huge headache, so I asked her for some water. She left and brought back a small glass of it, along with some crackers and cheese. The first officer returned to the room with some forms and a camera. He sat down and started filling out the form, asking questions while comparing my answers to the information on my passport. I quickly thought it would be a good idea to tell them about a couple of alterations we had made to the passport.

"I had to make some alterations to the original passport," I told them.

"Why did you have to do that? You are holding a valid passport!" the woman said. I told her that I made the changes out of fear of being stopped at the airport and said I had thought I would have a better chance of getting out if I used a falsified document. They seemed not to care about what I told them; they just continued to write and fill out the forms. I did not know then what my fate was going to be, but I felt like I had a chance of staying, as they never bothered to ask about my connecting flight and valid visa to Austria. I reasoned that they would not have allowed me to wait here and miss my next flight if they did not plan to grant asylum.

"Do you have your friend's phone number?" the woman asked. I wanted to jump out of my chair as I told her yes and reached for my wallet. She noted the number and after a pause asked me to follow her to the next room. She then dialed the number and handed me the phone. I was happy but apprehensive! What would I do next if Homayoun or one of his family did not answer? Fortunately, Homayoun's wife answered the phone and I immediately told her it was me.

"How wonderful, you are here; we actually talked about you during dinner last night," she mentioned. I told her where I was and that they wanted to talk to Homayoun.

"He just went out for grocery shopping, but I know where he is and will get hold of him right away."

"My friend is not home but will be available soon," I told the officer as I handed the phone back.

"Tell him to pick his friend from the airport police office," the officer told Homayoun's wife. After hanging up, she approached and shook my hand firmly.

"Welcome to Germany," she said with a smile. The male officer followed and welcomed me, too. It was quite a feeling at a time like this. I was very relieved and happy, not just for myself but for my entire family and the dream of rescuing everyone someday. I thought the door to future opportunities was opening; there was now a light at the end of the tunnel.

As I walked along with the two officers, I thanked them and told them how grateful I was. They led me to a waiting room and told me to report to Schöneck refugee camp within two days. After waiting a couple hours there, where I was served chips and soda, I heard my name called and was quickly led to a door leading to the airport's main lobby, where I saw Homayoun waiting anxiously with a big smile on his face.

As we took the escalators down to the train station, I felt disoriented and completely puzzled by the flow of people, flashing commercials, structures, buildings, and modern life. I had never traveled out of Afghanistan at that point, so, while everything looked fascinating, I also felt overwhelmed by my new surroundings. On the train, Homayoun told that he would take me to a hotel where he and his family were staying temporarily with several other Afghan families and would then take me to join his nephew Atiq later that night. I was glad to hear about Atiq, as he was a great friend and former coworker at the Hotel Inter-Continental, too.

"Don't worry, Frankfurt is full of Afghans," Homayoun said. "They are arriving by the hundreds every day." He said he had gone to the airport three times a week to welcome a friend or someone he knew.

When we arrived at the hotel, Homayoun's wife had graciously prepared a nice dinner for all of us. After we chatted and reminisced, it was time to go to Atiq's home, where I would spend a couple nights before reporting to Schöneck refugee camp.

"You are free from communist rule. It is time to celebrate," said Atiq, as we went out to explore the city the first night.

# Lost Decency

There it was: Frankfurt. I was once again completely overwhelmed by structures, skyscrapers, lighted buildings, and the sight of people all over. I had never been exposed to such a lifestyle as I was while we walked through the crowded streets of Frankfurt's downtown area. To be exposed to such a flashy, modern city was quite an experience for someone who had not traveled outside Afghanistan.

After a couple of nights of visiting with friends, it was time to face the realities of life as a refugee. It sounded and felt awkward indeed. I had never imagined becoming a refugee one day and being away from my homeland, so the anxiety of beginning this new phase of life was starting to sink in.

Homayoun and his family, along with many Afghan families, had been given housing at various hotels and residences around Frankfurt, but the rush of refugees had so overwhelmed the German government that a refugee distribution center within the small city of Schöneck had been arranged. The refugees arriving at that time in Europe and other countries were well-educated, middle-class professionals who had run away because they either worked within the government or were not willing to support it, and therefore posed a threat to the communist regime.

Some of these educated Afghan refugees in other countries were considered well qualified to become doctors in hospitals or lecturers at universities and humanitarian support organizations in places such as Iran and Pakistan. Many with good entrepreneurial skills started to open import-export businesses and other firms, which became attractive to neighboring countries. However, it was a completely different situation in Europe.

I remember asking Homayoun if we had a chance to work, instead of sitting home all day, while we were refugees. He laughed, but was quick to respond with anger and frustration: "I wish that was the case; that is exactly what we thought, too, when we arrived. You can work a little, but only illegally."

I asked him what that meant.

He again smiled and said, "Refugees are not allowed to work until they get accepted as legal residents; they better not find out you are working before that, or you will be kicked out quickly." He continued, "You are no longer at the Hotel Inter-Continental, Atta. You are now a refugee." The word "refugee" felt disturbing.

"What has become of us? This is so sad," I sighed, and we wept together for a good few minutes.

ᴥᴥᴥ

Homayoun was kind enough to travel with me by train and drop me off at the big Schöneck refugee camp, which was a former army facility with many housing units and the amenities of a military base. This place was not a permanent refugee camp; it served simply as a refugee assessment and distribution center. As I walked through the compound toward the registration office, I was greeted by a few other Afghans, who offered to carry my bag in a true Afghan manner and tradition. It felt like being home and welcomed by family or friends.

That feeling that I was not alone was probably the most settling and friendly experience I could have had within a foreign land. It just felt wonderful to be in the company of my own people. Within minutes I had been registered and given a room, which I had to share with a couple of Afghan men, a doctor and his younger brother, who had come from Romania. These two gentlemen were the brothers of two great Afghan soccer players, so I was quite happy to be their roommate because we could talk about football. They later learned about my close association with Afghan football and about my younger brother, who had also been a member of the national team for a short time.

This new group of about three hundred had gathered inside a big cafeteria to learn about our food and other welfare benefits for the first time. We had been instructed the night before to report early that day. As we reluctantly entered the hall, we walked slowly through the crowd with a sense of guilt and shame, often looking up at the people around us just to see who was there. We noticed elderly people, families with very young kids, adults, and lots of women and children in general—people of all ranks and classes. Not a single person looked happy, and many preferred to look down as if they had committed a crime or were feeling guilt and betrayal. Even without shackles or armed guards, and despite the civil and good conditions, we somehow felt like victims of war, similar to scenes from World War movies and history pictures.

We were called up one at a time to a table, where authorities started handing out food vouchers, as well as some cash. We were then given information about grocery shops within the area and were instructed to stay within a five-mile radius and not to venture out until permanent relocations were announced.

Within this compound, refugees were to cook their own food and shop from local stores. While it was easy and preferable for Afghan families to cook their own food, it was quite a struggle for the single Afghan men. It's safe to say that about 99 percent of Afghan men at the time did not know how to cook or prepare their meals. When I returned to my room, the doctor told me with a grin, "Now you must cook for us!" I looked at him with surprise as I tried to figure out why he thought I knew how to cook. He quickly smiled and said not to worry. "You two do the shopping and wash the dishes and clothes; I will do the cooking! I know how," he said.

"Oh, thank God!" I sighed and told him I had no idea how to cook but would be happy to help and do the dishes. We then set out together to go shopping at the closest grocery within walking distance, where, for the first time, we experienced a modern German store. Completely lost and overwhelmed and not understanding a single German word, I simply followed my roommates and listened for their instructions. The doctor and his brother acted as though they knew German and were more familiar with the conditions because of their stay in Europe, and they started picking various items from the shelves and tossing them into the cart. I had no idea what these items were, but warned them that I would not touch anything that had pork in it. The younger brother laughed sheepishly as we continued down the aisle.

When we separated for a moment, I picked up a stack of wrapped cheese and started to look for any English word. I knew this was some sort of cheese but was anxious to start a conversation with someone, so I looked at a middle-aged woman and asked her in English if this was indeed cheese. She looked me with a big frown and disgust as she kept on walking past me into the aisle.

"What is her problem?" I asked my roommate. He told me right away told me that Germans didn't like to speak English and didn't care for foreigners at all. My friend Homayoun had warned me a little bit about the same thing earlier, but I was just trying to make sure. I did not like to hear about such treatment, as I had built quite a good impression about foreigners in Afghanistan, and since at home we treated foreigners as our own guests.

But I realized it wasn't just that lady. Every other person looked at us with disgust and obvious anger. Later that evening, I asked my elder roommate about our experience at the store, and about the fact that Germans did not like us. He went on to explain that overall

Germans were extremely protective of their country and did not care for foreigners much, despite the German government's openness to the flood of Afghan refugees.

"Idiots!" the doctor started to shout.

"You are both young, but I wanted to tell you that our own Afghan government during King Zahir Shah refused an opportunity to allow this labor agreement between Afghanistan and Germany. This was ours, but they gave it away," my roommate continued, with anger in his voice.

"There would now have been millions of us living here like Turks; plus, we would have built our country as these people did," he went on to say with much frustration. He told us that the Afghan government had simply given up on the idea because of idiotic and stubborn nationalistic ideals, when Germany called for deployment of at least two million Afghans as laborers to Germany at the time.

"This is yet another example of the neglect and incompetence that have put us in today's condition," my roommate said.

# Bubbles in the Kitchen

After spending a couple days in the Schöneck refugee compound, I met some more friends at the soccer grounds inside the camp, which had become the main attraction for many refugees. We gathered every afternoon and played several rounds of games. I then found a few people from our own neighborhood in Kabul, including one man named Omar, who invited a bunch of us to his apartment for dinner one night.

We arrived at Omar's apartment after a pickup game of soccer one night and found him and a couple of his roommates outside their apartment, holding their tummies as they laughed madly. I had never seen anyone laugh so hard and so loud before and wondered what had happened.

One of our friends said, "They must be drunk."

Omar responded swiftly, while still laughing, "No we are not; something very funny has occurred." I asked him to tell us, but they kept on laughing and started waving us toward their room.

"Wait," he said, as he put his hands up to stop us at the door of the room. "You are going go to die." He continued to laugh.

He then opened the door. The room was blanketed with a layer of white foam.

"What happened?" asked one of the refugees.

"We purchased and used dishwasher soap instead of oil," said one of the occupants of the room. "We poured a large amount into the dishwasher and left for just a few minutes, but the whole thing blew up and turned into foam," he explained, as he laughed loudly.

"But that is nothing—thank God we had to look at the entire purchase and realized we had also bought dog food in cans instead of regular beef . . . ha ha ha ha." He was by then laughing so hard that tears were coming out of his eyes.

We all started laughing with them, then started to help clean the kitchen floor and oven, as the white foam had spread throughout the apartment. After that great laugh, we had a fun night of reminiscing and talking into the early hours of morning. Staying up late at night and waking up late in the morning was by then a way of life within the Schöneck refugee camp.

৶৶৶৶৶৶

After a week's stay, we learned that it was actually possible to leave the camp area—dozens of refugees would sneak out and go to Frankfurt and other cities to visit friends or go shopping—but it was a risky move, as capture by police could jeopardize their status and eligibility for permanent visas.

After two anguished months of boredom, it was time to find out about our future homes. It was a big day for many, as their next destination would could become their permanent home. We were once again summoned to the big cafeteria, with our belongings packed and ready for departure. The lobby inside looked more like an airport. We were informed that refugees would be going to seven different

125

areas of Germany, so my hope again was to be closer to friends in Frankfurt or Paderborn, in the north. We learned that they were no longer allowing refugees within the Frankfurt area, and I and thirteen other men were called to gather in a corner of the big hall, where a camp employee was waiting with a list in his hand. As we approached, the gentleman asked if any of us spoke German or English.

No one stepped up and volunteered himself as German-speaking, but I raised my hand and told the man that I spoke English. He then called me to the front row and told me in English that this group would be going to Mahlberg, Euskirchen. I then turned and told the group about this location and asked if anyone knew where this city was. No one seemed to have any idea, so I asked the officer if Mahlberg was close to any of the major cities. He then informed me that Euskirchen was somewhere between Bon and the city of Koln and that it was a very beautiful area. The officer went on to tell us that families with children were being designated to cities where more Afghans were concentrating and that we would be the first refugees in this particular city.

I was then instructed to help guide this group and communicate with the driver and the authorities in the receiving town of Mahlberg. The group reluctantly started to gather their belongings and headed toward a waiting bus outside the refugee compound, filled with disgust and uncertainty.

"What in the world has happened to us?" cried out an old man from behind the bus. He shouted loudly that he had not had any news from his family and now he was going to be moving even further into isolation and away from people he knew in the Frankfurt area, as he continued to weep. We all realized that living within a big camp full of fellow countrymen and families had brought us a sense of peace, security, and closeness, and that we now had to deal with the prospect of living away from our own Afghans for the rest of our lives.

It was deathly silent as the bus moved away from Schöneck. Except for the occasional sigh, no one was willing to talk out loud, although some cried openly or chatted quietly with their neighbors.

After several stops to drop off smaller groups in various cities, we were getting close to our new home destination. The driver called my name and asked me to move to the front of the bus and take a seat there. He started to explain that we would soon be leaving the metropolitan areas and would climb into a beautiful mountainous area. He was right; the scenery was getting prettier and prettier. We spotted picturesque villages across the highway, and mountains topped with snow. "That is Euskirchen," the driver yelled. We looked ahead and spotted a town embedded in a valley of amazing beauty.

"But we are not going to live there, are we?" we asked. "What about Mahlberg?"

The driver said, "Mahlberg may be a village within this city. You will like the area, but I don't believe you will find a single refugee here. I have been told that your group is going to be the first to land in this area. Could be good or could be bad." He smiled widely.

I honestly had no idea what to make of his statement and reaction but realized that people of this area would not welcome us with open arms. Still, it might be good for our group, as we would be away from the hustle and bustle of the big cities and might be better off in a remote area, leading a simpler life. Unlike the group and most other refugees, I preferred to be in a quiet location, away from all the noise and big crowds.

As the bus pulled in front of the city hall, the driver asked that we wait until he got instructions from the city authorities. Within minutes, he emerged along with a tall, professionally dressed woman who stepped inside the bus and introduced herself as the caretaker of the group. She spoke in clear English and had a very kind demeanor, so we were truly happy to have her welcome us. She informed us that it would be a fifteen-minute drive to our destination, Mahlberg. As she sat next to me, she extended her hand and introduced herself as Ingrid Bower.

I in turn introduced myself but told her I did not know any of the people within this group. She seemed genuinely happy but also a little nervous.

"Is this true that we are the first refugee group in this area?" I asked.

She smiled and said that there had actually been a couple of refugees from one of the Asian countries in the past, but they had left the area. So we were indeed the first group of refugees from Afghanistan; Mahlberg had never in its history seen any refugees before. I then asked about Mahlberg as we drove up the hills and into gorgeous mountains covered with greenery and trees.

"We believe Mahlberg is a nice village with very nice people," she said, as we got closer to the edge of the village and looked anxiously around the area. The bus slowed down significantly as we started to enter the village, but more fear and anxiety surrounded our group, as we could not see a single human movement outside. The place truly looked like a ghost town.

"Does anyone live here?" one of the group members yelled from behind the bus.

I repeated it as I looked at Ingrid. She looked embarrassed and annoyed. "Sure, there are about five hundred people in this village."

By that time, the entire group was crowding against the windows as they looked outside. We then noticed a couple of open windows as people snuck to see the arrival of the Afghans.

"Wow, look, they just closed their door—look at the left! Another woman is closing her window!" This really reminded me of some cowboy Westerns I had seen in the past where scared villagers nervously prepared themselves for the arrival of invaders and bandits.

"Look, there is an old man looking from his window," yelled someone from the back of the bus.

We were truly disturbed and sad about these sights, and wondered how this group could ever make it here. Ingrid continued to instruct the driver as he made several turns through the village and finally turned toward the highest area of the village, stopping in front of the very last house at the end of the road. There was nothing but silence as Ingrid stood and pointed to the house on the right as our next home. It was a huge old house overlooking a beautiful landscape and farmland, but with no walls or fences. It seemed as if no one had lived there for a long time.

It was very quiet, and we still could not see a single soul on the street or anyone even inside the nice farmhouse just across from our big house, but somehow we knew the residents were peeking from inside their homes, so it was a disgusting feeling.

"Are you sure people live here?" I asked Ingrid as we got off the bus.

She said, "Absolutely, they will come out." As she led us into the big house, the entire group started unloading their belongings and gathered for a meeting with her.

"Please just put your luggage in the lobby and come into the big living room," she said.

She then asked how many people spoke or understood English. A few more raised their hands, and she asked them if it was okay that I was representing the group. Everyone nodded, as they all realized I spoke English fluently.

"I am sorry for what had happened to you and your country," she said. "I have been reading day and night since my assignment as your worker, so I feel for you, and I am truly sorry for the reaction of people of this village." She then told us that the villagers had been informed a couple weeks earlier about our potential move and they were indeed upset, not because of us specifically but because of accepting refugees in general. She said this village had never in its history since World War II been home to any refugee, so it might take a while for the people to adjust.

She went on to talk about our next steps, saying that we needed to go to the city to learn about support, food, and other instructions for our life as refugees. She also informed us about a supply of food that had been prepared for the entire group for the next two days, until we were ready to shop for and make our own meals.

But what about our big concern about these people in the village? I asked Ingrid if they knew exactly who we were and why we had become refugees, and whether it was possible to arrange for a meeting with the elders and people of the village. Ingrid also seemed visibly disappointed by the reaction of the villagers, so she was quite amused at the gesture, and said, "Sure, I know quite a few people in this village, and it is an excellent idea." She told us that she would send a bus the next day to get us to the city, but we would be on our own in the future.

As she said goodbye that evening, Ingrid mentioned that the refugee authority had assigned seven rooms to our group of fourteen, so each person would end up with a roommate. The building had only two bathrooms, but it had a central heating system, so it actually felt quite comfortable as we roamed around the house.

It was then time for the group to get to know each other and start room assignments. As the group leader, I did not think it was a good idea to assign rooms randomly, so I suggested that we sit down around the table, introduce ourselves, and figure out the best match-up in terms of personalities. In a matter of minutes, we realized we had a mix of very educated people from various walks of life, including two teachers, a mechanic, and a professional chef. That was the best news of all: we had a chef who could lead the way, or at least teach us how to cook.

The group was very engaging, except for one man, who looked like an Afghan but did not have the demeanor and attitude of one, and who spoke sparing and dialectical Pashto. He started speaking in fluent Pashto and told the group he did not speak Farsi or Dari, but that he had come from a village in the south of Afghanistan. He also informed us that he did not wish to share a room with anyone, due to his medical condition.

We decided to suggest roommates based on age groups. I started to speak to the man in Pashto, but he rambled in a very different dialogue, so the group felt like this man was probably not an Afghan and had only pretended to be one in order to make it here as a refugee. This would not have been out of the ordinary, since Pashto-speaking nationals of Pakistan might have wanted to seek refuge in another country, and this was a time when Afghan refugees were being widely accepted. Some people would pay a significant amount of money to enter a country under a different nationality.

After several discussions and heated arguments, we decided to put a group of three in a bigger room and assign this man a single room in the house for the time being. I offered to join the other two men and take a bigger room. After spending time in Schöneck and getting used to roommates within even smaller units, I did not find this a difficult decision, as we were now inside a bigger house within a quiet village. I was actually happy to get away from big, cosmopolitan cities and crowds in general. Being driven farther into isolation somehow felt better; I simply wanted to lead a peaceful life as I tried to plan my next move as a refugee away from my loved ones for now.

# German Pastry

As we were getting ready to go to the city the next day, we heard our doorbell. We wondered who would ring it, considering our disappointment about our first impression of the villagers and their reaction to our arrival. No one else wanted to interact with the villagers, so I and another member of the group hurried to see who was behind the door.

It was a woman with a big smile, along with her husband and a young German boy. The woman was holding a box wrapped in plastic.

"Hello," she said.

I returned the greeting.

"*Ich* Elizabeth," she said, probably realizing we did not speak German at all; by then most at least know what *ich* meant.

Her husband then extended his arm and I shook his hand. "*Ich bin* Kurt."

I responded in English, "I am Atta," as they looked at us with broad smiles on their faces. I pointed toward the entryway and welcomed them inside. By then most of the other guys had come closer to the entryway and were eager to welcome their first German guests. As we sat around the table, Elizabeth started speaking in German to her young son.

After a long pause, the boy said, in broken English, "I am Mario. I speak a little English, but my parents do not. We are here to say hello and welcome you; our house is just opposite yours. That one," he said, and pointed through the window to the house on the opposite side of the street. It was a very nice one-story home with a big plot of land right behind it, so it was obvious they were farmers.

I told Mario to thank his parents and tell them how happy we were to have such nice neighbors. The couple kept on smiling genuinely as they looked around.

"My mother baked this cake for you just this morning," the young boy mentioned, almost whispering. I thanked them again on behalf of the group and apologized to them for not having any tea or snack that we could offer them. I also informed them that we were waiting for the bus so that we could register as residents of this area, and that we would for sure have some tea or snacks next time they were in our home.

The boy laughed as he spoke to his parents, and they all started laughing. It was an incredibly touching moment, but it was also extremely frustrating for them and all of us that we could not communicate properly. It was, however, a great turn of events in starting to communicate and build relationships with the people of this small village.

As we got on the bus and looked down the street, there were actually a few people around, going about their daily business—unlike the night before, when the whole village had shut down their doors and windows upon our arrival. We later went through a tedious process of registration and a long wait at the social services office in Euskirchen, where we were handed food stamps, cash, and vouchers for clothing; I believe each of us got the equivalent of US$400 in deutsche marks at the time toward clothes.

We were also warned that we were under no condition allowed to leave the twenty-five-mile radius of Euskirchen as we tried to explore our transportation options, grocery stores, and other necessities of refugee life within this small but hostile environment.

Strange indeed! Living in big and metropolitan cities is a lot different from living in a small town where refugees are not welcome and frowned at every moment. We were visibly the big news in town. We felt like wild animals inside a cage—no matter where we were, people of all ages not only could not take their eyes off us, but continued to mumble words that none of us could understand. The ugly stares of the middle-aged and older men and women were quite obvious and upsetting, as some would look until we disappeared from their eyesight.

"My goodness, I can't take this!" a member of our group cried in total frustration.

"Do they know what people all around Afghanistan are feeling and going through and why we are here?" another refugee questioned.

"I would rather be dead and buried there than here. Are you paying attention around you? Look, they look at you like you have killed someone," said the youngest member of the group, who had left his studies after only one year of college.

"And what about the people in the village? Are you sure we can make it?" He kept on asking questions loudly. He eventually broke into tears as we gathered around him to calm him down before we headed as a group to a big discount grocery store.

Within a few days, Ingrid had called to inform us that she had arranged for us to meet with the elders and local officials of Mahlberg during an evening event. This was the big moment we had been waiting for, as we had completely isolated ourselves within the house and the small area around leading to the hills, fearing a hostile confrontation with anyone. We had also recently heard about some horrible incidents of attacks all over Germany by skinheads and neo-Nazis, so we were especially apprehensive about our situation. I had the entire group prepare themselves by dressing up and looking sharp in order to make a statement about our past status and the fact that we had been forced to leave our homeland and were not in Mahlberg to seek a job or better living, but rather to find safety.

I also made sure Ingrid and other representatives from social services were going to be present as we met the villagers. Upon Ingrid's arrival with a couple other city officials, we made our way to a town hall large enough to accommodate hundreds of people. We had thought we might meet with a handful of villagers, so we were completely surprised to find over one hundred people of all ages: elders, women and men, and quite a few youth.

"We are a big deal here, then," mentioned one of the refugees. I told him this was truly great news because it meant we could make a good statement. Ingrid had informed me before the meeting that the people of this village were determined to sign a petition to protest our arrival here in Mahlberg, and had once again mentioned that never in the history of this village had any foreigner lived here. She politely linked this to the geography of the area, saying that the German government had had no reason to place anyone in such a remote location; she wanted us to understand people's reaction and their feelings.

After briefly introducing herself in German, Ingrid announced that she would serve as a translator and mediator. She then called my name to come up and make our statement. At that point I felt very energized and ready to tell them what had happened to us as a nation, hoping to enlighten this community, separated from the rest of the world and living in its own little bubble. I provided a brief but proud history of Afghanistan and its people, and of the emergence of communism and ultimate invasion of Afghanistan by Russia. I made references to certain former Soviet invasion victims, such as Poland and other Eastern European countries, as well. I informed them about the massacre of millions of people and the flood of refugees fleeing and seeking shelter all around Afghanistan, Europe, and America, and the fact that we had no intention other than to simply run away from the atrocities of the communist regime in hopes of saving our and our families' lives.

There was complete silence as the villagers listened intently to my speech. After about half an hour I paused and asked if they had any questions for us, and mentioned that I hoped they would be honest and up-front in terms of acceptance and understanding of our situation. I then briefly introduced each member of the group, along with their marital status and the fact that several of these folks had been victims of torture and imprisonment and placed on a government watch list, so they had left behind their families and children in hopes of rescuing them someday.

"Do you know how long you will be here?" was the first question, from a well-dressed, middle-aged man. I told him we had no idea, and that the authorities had not mentioned anything to us. He then went on to say he was a computer engineer and that he would be happy to help find jobs for us. That was a huge surprise, and a big morale boost.

"Would you be willing to learn German, then?" he asked.

I told the group that it would be indeed a great idea for us to learn the language, as we were at a huge disadvantage at this point. The crowd was visibly warming up to us, and then came the turn of our neighbor, Elizabeth. She moved from her chair and closer to the podium as she prepared to talk. She started talking in German, of course, with visible enthusiasm and happiness. I whispered to Ingrid to ask if her remarks could be translated, as it was important for the group to understand what was being discussed about us.

We were informed that Elizabeth had told the group that she had had a memorable first visit at our home and had brought us a cake she and her husband had prepared, and that she got a great impression about our group. She asked the villagers to welcome and accept us in their community.

It was then time for the president of the village chamber of commerce, Mr. Kohn, to speak. He was a retired army officer who had served in World Wars I and II. Mr. Kohn spoke with authority and firmness as he told the crowd about his deep respect for Afghan people, sharing a story of his visit to Afghanistan in the early '60s, along with a group of Germans.

He told the group that he had almost forgotten about his early visit to Afghanistan, but the events of the last few years and the Russian invasion had refreshed his memory, and that he was extremely angry about the invasion. He told the crowd that he would take personal responsibility for our well-being, and challenged the villagers to embrace the new refugees in their village. We felt truly thankful for his honest and straightforward comments, which gave us a huge lift. He then walked from his seat and came to shake our hands one by one. More and more villagers then stood and came to exchange greetings as they welcomed us. This was a huge victory, and we all breathed a sigh of relief. We would never have gotten so much support if we had stayed quiet and not met with the people of this village.

The next day we were featured in both village and Euskirchen newspapers, which made reference to our meeting, as well as the reasons for our stay in this area as refugees. The articles went on to expand upon the war and the Russian invasion in particular. We were quite happy with the outcome, and kept trying to make the necessary adjustments for acceptance within our new environment.

The villagers had truly opened their hearts and minds to us. Within days, they delivered various home items, including a video game system and a ping-pong table, which soon became our most popular activity. As we started roaming around the area more freely, we found that Mahlberg was indeed a beautiful village; it sat on top of rolling hills and farmland, and was surrounded by rugged forests and trees. The view from our home and into the valley was quite stunning. We knew it was only a matter of time before we felt used to our new surroundings.

Many of the residents were farmers, so our group decided to just get out there and simply offer to help with little chores. We thought that was a good way to break through, and a means of exercising and making the best of our time. Some joined in helping the residents without speaking a word of German; oftentimes we used English words and sign language as we tried to integrate ourselves into the community.

Our other activities consisted mainly of walking to surrounding towns and cities, playing cards, playing football, cooking, and reading. A couple of the boys from the group joined the village's competitive soccer team, and the majority would play almost every day. We had by then attracted several boys from the village who would come play soccer with us right in our own big backyard, which had no walls and headed down straight to the wooded area about a quarter of a mile below.

Evenings turned grim, as all of would gather to listen to BBC and other English or Persian radio channels for news about our country. At the time, none of us had any direct communication with anyone inside Afghanistan through regular mail, except for the occasional letter delivered to family members. I personally had not had any direct communication with anyone at home since arriving in Germany, except for the word-of-mouth notice of my arrival through friends who had been in Germany for a while and had established mail communication with their families. So I knew my family was aware that I had made it here safely. Otherwise, none of us had any idea what was happening to our families and loved ones, so keeping busy was crucial to our survival and positive state of mind.

# Sweep the Cemetery!

WITHIN A FEW DAYS OF OUR ARRIVAL, we received a call from the social services office telling us that someone was going to visit us in our residence, so we anxiously waited for the arrival of the social services representative. Life as a refugee is oftentimes filled with anxiety and fear of the unknown, and was so particularly at the time, as we had heard about false reporting and accusations of being tagged as members of the Communist Party or other subversive political movements; everyone feared interrogations, or even potential deportation. Once again, it was time to wait and see.

After a long, tension-filled weekend, Ingrid arrived with a man who introduced himself as a member of the city municipal works. After a brief introduction, Ingrid told us that we would be required to work within city limits for periods of twenty to thirty hours a week in return for cash and food stamps.

Everyone seemed stunned and quite annoyed, but at the same time happy, that the meeting had nothing to do with our fear of false reporting of any suspicious activity within our group. It was, however, time to fear the quality of the work, based on stories coming out of other refugee camps about harsh public-works jobs such as cleaning highways, sweeping city streets and parks, etc.

The group asked me to find out about the type of work we were going to be required to do. We were told it was working in public parks, which would include road construction, cleaning, and sweeping. Well, we had no choice but to at least try and see what kind of work we were going to be asked to perform. We were then given instructions to bring our own food and told about where and when to report the next day.

After another anxious night, the entire group had to wake up very early in order to be in the city by 8:00 AM. That was no easy task, as most of the group had gotten lazy, refugee-style, by sleeping late, and the fact that we had only two bathrooms for fourteen people meant we had to get up much earlier to get the whole group ready.

We arrived at the job site, which looked like a big city maintenance yard with lots of equipment and cars, and were immediately led to a waiting bus. On that bright and beautiful fall day, we drove for about ten minutes and then arrived at a huge public park right below gorgeous hills, with big trees and most of the ground covered with fallen leaves, where we were handed yellow plastic jackets and gloves. It was a grim moment; it felt like we, too, were innocent victims of nature and were about to be swept away by its force.

After we stood there in silence for several minutes and waited for instructions, a man in his fifties came and started talking in German to the group. We did not understand exactly what he was saying, so I asked him if he could tell us in English what to do.

"*Scheisse!*" he shouted as he kept on talking in a loud voice, in a very upsetting manner. He then realized we did not understand any of the words, so he started to point to our yellow jackets to indicate that we should put them on, and asked us to follow him to a small building. He opened the gate and handed us brooms and shovels.

He then shouted, "Groups!" and pointed to smaller groups while using his hand to signal the direction we had to go; eventually we realized he meant groups of two working in various areas of the park. As we gathered together to form small groups, a couple of people got upset and asked if they could be excused from this duty. I told them that this man did not understand any English, and, more important, what would we accomplish by refusing to follow instructions as refugees? What choice did we have? I personally did not see a reason or way to refuse, but still, I told them it was their decision.

"What can you do?" I asked.

A young man named Naim said, "Well, we can hire an attorney."

I said that, too, was an option, but that he needed to figure out how he could obtain the money to do so. I asked him if he actually knew anyone who could find him an attorney.

Another member of the group spoke up and said, "Why don't we launch a strike?"

"Others have done so, but to no avail," shouted another member, who then talked about his cousin's experience and the fact that his friends had been working on road construction projects and sweeping parks might not be a bad idea. "I think this is the easier assignment; I have a feeling it will get worse," he said.

An older member, Aziz, the professional chef of the group, told us we were wasting time and there was no reason for us to refuse.

"We have lost our country and plan to save our and our families' lives here. You are not invited here, and are not guests; you are only refugees," he said. Everyone seemed to respect and listen to that, and we split into smaller groups and started sweeping the leaves.

As we began moving in different directions, I realized how quiet and subdued my fellow refugees were, heads down and some simply wiping tears off their faces as they reluctantly swept.

"My God, we have reached a German cemetery," called a member of the group as he retreated from his work area. "It's true, they have us clean the cemeteries, too," he shouted with disgust and anger in his voice. The whole group moved toward the area and looked around the fenced yard full of graves, stunned and frustrated. A teacher started sobbing as he held his head with his two hands. Everyone then started crying as well, some sitting down or on their knees and looking down, but no one dared to say anything. It was completely silent for a few minutes. Naim, who had left Afghanistan during his second year of engineering school of Kabul University, was the most distraught and disappointed of all; he cried nonstop as we hugged him and moved him away from the area. The entire group then stopped working, and we put the jackets and equipment away.

We had been in the area for about three hours, so we had no way of leaving the place by ourselves since we had no access to transportation. The man in charge had left and was supposed to check up on us, but there was no sign of him anywhere. We did not wish to venture away, as we did not want to jeopardize our status, so there was no option but to wait. We gathered again as a group and talked about our frustrations and the fact that no one had any contact with members of their family at the time, and about how we were devastated and were getting more and more disappointed each day. This latest assignment to sweep the park and cemetery was the last bit of bad news the group did not need.

After a couple of hours, the man arrived in his truck; he started walking toward us with obvious anger as he saw the whole group gathered without our yellow jackets and not working. He again started shouting and rambling in German. I started yelling in English and told him that we would not sweep the cemetery, while pointing toward the area and crossing my arms in a gesture of telling him, *No work there*. We then saw him calm down and apparently understand that we were not happy to sweep the cemetery, so he pointed at us to gather the equipment as he telephoned someone to send the bus.

Ingrid called me first thing the next morning and asked what had happened. I told her how frustrated and insulted everyone was and said our group was not willing to go back to this park or be sent to another cemetery. She promised to talk to her boss right away and recommend a different type of work. We anxiously waited for almost a whole week and then were informed that we would be helping with road construction jobs from now on. We were off to this new job within a week. This was very hard work, which consisted of drilling, carrying heavy loads, and mixing up cement. Working side by side with German and Turkish workers was no easy task, in light of their sometimes demeaning attitude, language, and treatment, but we realized we did not have many options, and that we no longer were in control of our destiny.

# In Pursuit of
# the American Dream

$\backsim\!\curvearrowleft\!\backsim\!\curvearrowleft\!\backsim\!\curvearrowleft\!\backsim\!\curvearrowleft$

A COUPLE MONTHS INTO OUR STAY in Mahlberg, and after facing various challenges, I realized Germany was not a place for me to live. Afghan refugees in general lived and carried on with their lives through lots of frustration; despite the more adequate living conditions than in Afghanistan, they would prefer living with their families and seeing their country be free again of oppression, mass killing, and atrocities. The majority of us remained in Germany; some found their way to Austria, Italy, Holland, and other European countries; and others managed to apply and immigrate to the United States, but they could do so only if they had a close relative or if an international organization offered sponsorship.

My friend Homayoun had informed me that he and his family had been sponsored and accepted by a church and would be leaving for the United States within a few months. I asked him to take me to the same church in Frankfurt so I could apply for immigration to the United States as well. He had by then established an excellent relationship with the church, and was able to make an appointment for me. I went for an initial interview—which went very well, as I spoke good English and answered all their verbal and written questions—but they informed me that I should find a sponsor in the United States, since I was single and church and other human-rights organizations were mainly sponsoring families. I was actually quite happy to hear it, as I had several friends who had moved to the United States during the past few years. I thought of a very good friend of my brother who had lived in the Washington, D.C. area for a long time and had previously offered to sponsor me.

I happily called Younus and informed him I had made it to Germany and wanted to know if he would sponsor me. He graciously agreed and told me to apply right away, and he provided me with his address and all necessary information to fill out the forms. Within a couple days I was back in Frankfurt and officially applying for immigration to the United States. This was a big relief, until I realized that, sadly, this move had to be kept secret from my group of Afghans living in Germany. There were too many conflicting stories of abuse, sabotage, and espionage around, so it was best to just keep quiet until I was officially accepted.

I returned to our village to find that a big contractor had come to our home and informed the group that he would help us find jobs at his farm and in other farming areas. Most of the villagers were quite frustrated and did not agree with the government's plan to place all refugees on government aid. In several conversations, they had said they thought it would be best for us to work and earn income and not be a burden on society and taxpayers. We had also openly expressed our desire to work and not be on any type of welfare, so the villagers were not only in agreement but willing to help us. We were told that this contractor's offer would have to be kept a secret, though, as this was considered illegal work and the city and law enforcement would be all over the issue if they found out.

He had asked the group to make at least two or three people available every weekday for eight hours of work. We were able to come up with a schedule, and soon we were off to join this man for construction and farming work within our village and surrounding areas. This was a scary move, but we had no other option—we were badly in need of money. The aid provided by the government was barely enough to buy food and provide for transportation in and out of the village and city limits. While working for the contractor came with a big risk, it also felt quite safe, as he was very protective and oftentimes provided work within closed areas and away from the public eye. However, we stayed committed to attending construction jobs provided by the city in order to not cause any suspicion.

Travel outside the area was a risky decision; it often resulted in strong warnings and/or notations on personal records that would ultimately be a determining factor in whether people got permission to live in Germany or obtain permanent residency. Refugees had to be on their best behavior and do nothing foolish to attract a law enforcement officer on a train or bus. We had become aware of many incidents in which refugees were caught not having paid proper train or bus fare and without permission to travel outside of their designated area of living.

After a couple months I was informed by my friend Homayoun that his family had received their airline tickets and were getting ready to leave for the United States, so I decided to travel to Frankfurt to say goodbye. I made arrangements and carefully planned my trip, but I faced my biggest challenge on the way, only about a few miles away from Frankfurt. I was sitting at a window seat on the train when I noticed train officials entering the cabin. Ticket validation was an occasional routine; most people would simply show their ticket, but refugees and foreigners would more likely end up being asked for ID and permission to travel.

I quickly realized these officers were followed by armed policemen that day, so I knew they were looking for some suspicious activity. The two men approached a couple of people to my left, who seemed to be of Turkish descent, and one man starting screaming and tried to run for the door. He was quickly apprehended and handcuffed, along with his friend, as they continued to shout and curse in Turkish. The police and train officials then looked around and started asking everyone for IDs. I fortunately had my passport and city-issued ID and was ready to tell them about my plan to check on my immigration status with the church in Frankfurt.

"Passport?" one of the officers shouted. I handed him my passport, and he started browsing carefully through the pages. "Your travel permits?"

I knew then that I was in trouble. Refugees were occasionally allowed to travel with proper documentation and a good reason, but getting those permits was quite a hassle and often difficult. I told the officer that I had left the permit but was heading to the Lutheran church in Frankfurt for news of my travel to the United States. The two officers convened briefly and came back with a note stating that I needed to get a confirmation stamp from the church and mail it to their office or a notation will be made on my record.

I was very happy to do that, as I needed only to visit the church and ask for their blessing. The church director, Gertrude Shack, laughed loudly when I told her what had happened on the train to me. "This is so foolish—why they are limiting movements within our own country here?" she asked.

I asked her if there was a way to expedite my travel to the United States. After a short pause, she grabbed my file and told me to call within a week. I was so excited—somehow I had a very good feeling that I would get some good news from the church. Gertrude also asked me to inform German immigration authorities about my plan to immigrate to the United States if I was called for a hearing soon.

After about ten days, I called Gertrude from Euskirchen to find out if she had gotten any news about my status. She sound happy and informed me that my application had been approved, but that I would have to wait almost a year, as there were many cases pending and immigrant travels were very slow. I jumped with joy and could not contain myself inside the public phone booth as I screamed and kept on talking in Farsi to myself. As I strolled through the city's beautiful marketplace, I hummed and felt like a free man once again, ready to explore the world. It was indeed one of the happiest days of my life; I did not want to ride a bus back to the village, so I decided to simply walk, singing and feeling free, for a good ten miles through the beautiful valleys.

What a feeling! I was going to make it to America with a chance to rescue my family, but I knew that I could not afford to inform anyone besides my friend Homayoun and my sponsor in the United States, Younus. It was just too risky. That was just a fact of life as a refugee; I, along with all other Afghans, was learning and getting used to secrecy, deception, and being forced to hide simple facts of life. *How miserable*, I thought. *What about human innocence and decency*? I asked myself several times. *What happened to our beautiful and honest ways of life*? We had never had to look constantly over our shoulder before; life had been all about respect, love, honesty, integrity, and friendship until this point.

# Lost Decency

*What do Afghans have to do with Nuremburg?* I asked myself after receiving a notice to appear in court. Every refugee had to go through a rigorous interview/trial process in Germany, months, sometimes even years, after their arrival. The majority of these trials were held in Nuremburg. I did not know if the site of the notorious trials after World War II had been chosen by design, but its name did invoke fear and intimidation. These trials for refugees were the biggest and most feared events in our lives, as they steered the ultimate decision about whether we could stay or had to leave the country.

The government and law enforcement authorities were very precise and thorough with their investigation and research (similar to the process after 9/11 to determine immigrants' acceptance and/or deportation), so being granted asylum in Germany was no easy task. Some refugees would end up hiring attorneys if they were denied, and some would find a way to sneak out to a different European nation through smugglers. The smuggling and illegal entry of refugees from the Soviet Union and other former communist nations at the time was also rampant, so the German and other Western European governments had a very difficult job at hand.

Some good friends advised me not to share the news that I had been approved for U.S. immigration with anyone but German law enforcement and the Nuremburg trial authorities, and I was very apprehensive. These authorities had no legal power to stop me from traveling to the United States, but there was always the fear of sabotage and false reports at any time. Waiting for the trial was excruciating. It seemed like being worried about being rejected as a human being was becoming part of my daily life. I felt frustration about being away from my homeland, family, and friends, about the barrage of bad news I received about mass killings and destruction of homes, and about the uncertainty of not knowing where my future home was going to be.

༄༅༄༅༄༅

I was to report to Nuremburg at nine thirty in the morning for my trial. I anxiously left Euskirchen to make the five-hour trip by train. I was directed to check in to a hotel nearby, where I met quite a few Afghan families. I could see fear in almost everyone's eyes. I also thought it was important to look for people who had already completed their interview/trial, so that I could find out what kind of questioning and process they had gone through.

I was able to talk to a young fellow who also had been accepted to immigrate to the United States, and was very happy to meet him. He told me to simply inform the authorities, as soon as they started questioning me, that my request for immigration had been approved, and to show them my official letter. I had brought a copy with me, and I felt quite relieved, as I had heard some horror stories of people being denied even a short-term stay.

"My immigration request has been approved, and I will be going to America in within a few months," I told the translator, right after confirming my name, date of birth, and current address. He then turned to two judges, along with a third person, dressed in a police uniform. All the while, I was remembering World War movies and clips I had seen over the years, and thinking that I was right where many prisoners had been interrogated. It had the feeling and conditions of wartime interrogations, except for the lack of cruelty and physical abuse.

"Do you have the approval paper?" asked the translator. I reached into my pocket and pulled out the letter. This was the most important document I had ever had in my possession. I handed it over, and they started reading the letter, which was written in English.

"Good luck—you are done," the translator told me. They returned the letter as I thanked them. The whole process took only about five minutes, and was another big and happy moment, as I was starting to believe that I would indeed make to America. So now I thought it was time to return to the village and inform everyone about my approval to emigrate.

While my fellow refugees were happy for me, many were very visibly distraught to see me go, as we had become very close during our stay in Mahlberg and I had always been there to help them in many ways. eeeAfter being away from everyone, we had become a family. But I knew it was time to prepare to leave, as the church in Frankfurt had promised me a flight within the next few months.

A few weeks later, while opening the mail, I noticed an envelope from the church. I thought it was definitely an update about my travel. I opened the envelope in a hurry, and there it was: a short notice asking me to call the church as soon as possible. I ran to the phone and got hold of Gertrude. She told me that church management had decided not to send me to the United States before my sponsor's family arrived there. I knew this would be a challenge, as Younus's relatives had arrived in Germany as refugees after approval of my application; so this was not only a setback, but now there was no guarantee that I would even secure my sponsorship after their family was reunited in the United States.

While I felt really sad, I completely understood this dilemma, and wanted to see Younus's family go to the United States before me; I knew it would be very awkward if I arrived at his house before his own family. But I had no idea how much longer I had to wait.

I asked Gertrude if it was possible for me change sponsors, as I had lots of other friends in the United States, but she told me that would mean restarting the whole process and would probably take a good year more.

In the meantime, though, Younus found out about this latest challenge and personally approached the church authorities to request that they not delay my departure; I soon received another notice that my sponsor had in fact given them written permission to send me first, saying that his family would follow and asking for the process to follow its original course.

# Golden State

In October 1981, after almost two years of waiting, I received my departure confirmation via a letter from the church. I decided to simply travel around Germany during the next couple months, visiting friends, relatives, and former coworkers in various cities. I was a very happy guy.

I went to see a few of my former soccer teammates from Afghanistan. They were some of the former Afghan national team members who had secured political asylum in a famous international media event in Germany right after the Russian invasion of Afghanistan. Several of these men had made Paderborn their second home; most had remained active, and some had even made it onto Germany's second-division teams. They were a great bunch of young men with enormous talent who had been forced to leave their homeland and abandon their dreams.

On the day of my departure to the United States, I literally screamed, "I am going to America!" on the escalator at the Frankfurt airport. I could not stop whistling and humming, but I also could not shake a sense of anxiety, as, once again, nothing seemed to be guaranteed in life anymore.

"How much money are you taking with you?" asked an officer at customs. At first I had no idea why he asked me this question, but then I quickly remembered that the German airport police had recently seized a very large sum of cash from an Afghan family whom a smuggler had enticed to carry it to the United States. This poor family, with three young kids, had been arrested and turned away.

"I have only ten dollars in my pocket, officer. I am a refugee and have no more cash on me," I told him as I pulled my skinny wallet and handed to him. He opened it with a frown and stood up to check my pockets. How humiliating! Only suspicious people were subject to search those days.

All I wanted was to get on the plane and be on my way to America. Not until the woman at the ticket counter handed me my boarding pass did I feel like my dream was truly coming to fruition. As I boarded the plane, I was reminded of my previous walk to the airport in Kabul and how different that had felt. I remembered entering the plane with my head down, tears streaming down my face.

A waiting flight attendant said hello and offered to help me. "Are you okay?" she asked. I told her I was fine, and I kept on walking to my seat. I sat next to a nice American couple, and we politely exchanged greetings.

"First time going to America?" the man asked. I told him yes, and they both realized how distraught and overwhelmed I was.

"I am sorry. I am actually very happy, but I am just a little emotional," I explained. The distinguished-looking woman of the couple extended her hand and placed it on mine as she said, "Welcome to America."

"I am from Afghanistan and very happy to go to America," I said, then told them a little about my time in Germany, and the fact that I had left a big family behind in Afghanistan. From there, our conversation just took off, as they both showed enormous compassion and a very good knowledge of what had transpired in Afghanistan. The man told me immediately about his younger brother's fond memories of and experience in Afghanistan as a Peace Corps volunteer in the early '70s.

We talked on and off throughout the whole, nine-hour-long flight; I did not sleep for even a few minutes. I was still happy, but the thought of getting farther and farther away from home was too much to overcome.

As we got closer to the American shoreline, I could not take my eyes off the window. I felt as if I were about to step onto a different planet; I was eager to see skyscrapers, but I could see only beautiful coastal areas and beaches. I was so nervous that I could hardly relax.

My American travel companions were very gracious, and they told me they would walk me all the way to the customs area at Dulles International Airport. They even offered to take me to their home and said they would be happy to provide support and help if I needed it. It was as if we had known each other for a long time; they gave me a genuine sense of belonging and being welcomed in America. They helped me join the proper immigration line and then said goodbye, but assured me they would meet me in the lobby. They reminded me of very friendly Americans I had met over the course of my professional life and time back home.

After a short immigration process, I was greeted by my sponsor, Younus. I introduced him to the American couple, and we said our final goodbyes and headed straight out to an Afghan restaurant in the D.C. area. Younus jokingly mentioned that he was not a good cook, and said I might be hungry for some good Afghan food, which I was. As we drove away from the airport, I truly felt like I was watching an American movie! This city was beautiful, but nothing like what I had imagined. Somehow, I was expecting many high-rise buildings and crammed streets. I asked Younus if we were going to pass by many tall buildings. He laughed and said he liked it the way it was, but that I would see many tall buildings soon.

He then asked me right away if I planned to stay in D.C. He knew I had a lot of friends in the San Francisco Bay Area as well, but assured me I had his support if I planned to stay here with him. He did not want me to worry about his family and the fact that they would be arriving in the next few months.

I was actually quite happy to talk about my plans. I did not really know how and what to tell him about my future, but I thought I preferred to be closer to my friends in California. I thanked him again for his great support, and told him that I indeed had several high school and English classmates there. "I hope you don't mind," I said as I told him I would like to join my friends in California. He asked me to stay at least for a week so he could show me the D.C. area, even though it was very cold at the time and had actually snowed that evening. Younus then told me to take advantage of this time to apply for a Social Security card and get officially registered.

As I tried to get ready the next day to go out for a drive out and about in the area, I found a small envelope with my name on it. I opened the envelope and found quite a few $100 bills. *How does Younus know I have no money with me?* I thought. He was not only a smart man but very kind. I approached him and asked why he had left the money there. "That is just pocket money—let me know if you need more. That is one thing I don't want you to worry about until you get a job," he explained.

I told him my friends had already offered to send me airline tickets and I needed almost no money.

"Never mind. Pay me later, with interest," he said as he smiled and walked away.

"Many thanks," I told him. He smiled again and said money did not mean much and our friendship meant more than anything to him. He started to talk about my older brother and how proud Younus was to be his friend, and said he would do anything for our family.

Over the next two days, Younus took me around to show me the sights. While we explored, I found out about at least a thousand Afghans living in this area. Afghan communities traditionally stay close to each other, and Younus introduced me to several friends as we toured. The most intriguing, inspiring experience was driving and walking past the White House, the Abraham Lincoln memorial, and Arlington National Cemetery. I honestly could not believe that I had made it and was actually seeing these incredible sites from just a few hundred yards away.

The impact of being in D.C. for a week provided quite a motivation to appreciate life in the United States, and to work hard to give back. I continued to thank Younus for his support as he gave me excellent guidance about making the most of these opportunities.

After my stay in D.C., I was happy and felt energized to find a permanent home close to my schoolmates and coworkers in California. Of my many friends in the area, Homayoun, my first host in Germany, was the first to greet me.

"Amazing, ha, you cannot get rid of me," I told him as we drove away from the airport and on toward San Francisco.

"I am glad," he said. "This is what makes our friendship special, and this what friends are all about."

"Wow, I loved seeing the White House and some D.C.-area memorials, but this is real America," I said.

He looked at me and said, "Yes, now you are in California and Hollywood-land," as we passed through San Francisco and onto the Bay Bridge. I was completely overwhelmed once again, and occasionally I thought I was living in some fantasy.

"I got a place for you in our own city, very close to San Francisco," Homayoun said.

I was pleasantly surprised, as I had not known where I would be staying. I was excited about and thankful for the opportunity to be close to San Francisco. He said his nephew, Atiq—my friend from way back, with whom I had worked with at the Hotel Inter-Continental and then stayed for a few days in Frankfurt—was living in his same building, in a two-bedroom apartment in Alameda, and had happily agreed to welcome me as a roommate. Atiq had arrived in the United States a few months prior to my arrival.

Just imagine, living close to one of the most famous and beautiful cities in the world! "I am one of the luckiest people on Earth," I told Homayoun.

"You are right. I just wanted to stay alive, but here I am, actually working within the city and living close with my family," he said with a smile on his face. "We are indeed very lucky," he sighed.

I told him that I had no plans to stay home and be idle, and said I wanted to start working right away. He was happy to hear it and said there were opportunities around, but that I might have to start from scratch. "Our Afghanistan experience means nothing," he said. He told me had prepared a nice resume, filled with all of his hotel front-office experience, but he had still had to accept a reservations-operator position within one of the biggest hotels. He offered to let me know about any job openings at his workplace.

# The Storyteller

$\mathbb{W}$ITHIN MY FIRST WEEK in the Bay Area, several other friends reached out and started helping me with my search for a job. A good friend, Ahmad, told me the city was a good place to start. After talking and consulting with friends, I realized it was best to just hit the ground running in San Francisco. Ahmad gave me some excellent tips and told me use the *San Francisco Chronicle* as my main resource, but I was determined to not only look through classified ads but to just stop by corporate offices in person and visit their personnel departments. In the mornings, I would take an early bus from Alameda while carrying a small backpack containing snacks and comfortable shoes. I would start my search in the Embarcadero area and some days end up close to the opposite end of Market Street by simply walking and asking questions and looking for employment signs.

During my third day of searching, I found an ad for a "teller" position in the *Chronicle*. I honestly had no idea what the job was all about. I thought I had learned good English back home but had never heard the word "teller."

I called my friend Ahmad, who was a manager at a financial services company, to ask about the position. "I think I am quite bad at storytelling, so I don't think this is something for me."

He started laughing hysterically, and asked me to read him the advertisement. I told him it was a teller position with American Savings and Loan Association.

"You are so stupid," he said. "That is not a storytelling job, but rather a cashier type of position with a bank—that is my bank." He continued playfully, "Go there and see what happens, but try to speak clearly. You sound like thunder." He told me my voice was too deep and had a big accent, still laughing. We joked around a little, and I asked him about the address, posted as 10 Kearny Street. He started laughing again, corrected my pronunciation of "Kearny," and told me it was only a few feet away from where I was standing.

"But I am casually dressed and don't have a tie on," I said. I also told him I had blisters on my feet after walking up and down the San Francisco streets looking for a job. He said not to worry, but to just go in and say hello while inquiring about the position. "Tell them about your situation and just be up-front and honest; tell them that you have read about the position and are simply inquiring," he said.

I was starting to feel scared. I had no real cash-handling experience and knew banking was not the same as banking in Afghanistan, where I had obtained a few months' experience as a short-term typist at National Bank of Kabul after high school; but I kept Ahmad's advice about being up-front with them in mind, walked toward the bank building, and opened the door. I walked over to the desk of a gentleman who was dressed very professionally.

"Good afternoon, sir," the gentleman said as he looked up. "How may I help you?" I opened the newspaper and pointed to the ad and told him that I was interested in applying for that job. The man, who was in his fifties, realized right away that I was not a local and offered me a seat. I must have looked terrible, I realized later; I had not looked in a mirror since the early morning. I probably looked very tired, and was of course not dressed professionally.

"What is your name?" he asked.

I told him, "Attaullah, but they call me Atta."

"What is the origin of your name, young man?"

I told him I was from Afghanistan and had just arrived about a week ago.

"Do you have any bank experience?" he asked.

"I worked for the National Bank of Kabul as a typist for a few months," I told him. He started smiling, but was quick to realize I was very fresh from the ship and onto American soil, and that I needed help. He told me that banking was different in the United States, and he wished I had some cash-handling experience. I told him that I understood, but counting money would not be a problem for me. "Sir, I know what you are saying, but I am a quick learner and just need a chance. I know I can do this job."

"Tell me a little about yourself and what brought you here," he said, as he reached out for his pipe, which was sitting on his desk, and lit it. (There was no smoking ban in San Francisco at the time.)

"I left Afghanistan right after the Russian invasion and then went to Germany, where I waited for almost two years. I just came here as an immigrant last week."

"Did you learn English in Kabul?" I was happy to hear him mention our capital at least and realized he must have been keeping up with the Afghan story.

"Yes, I was actually born in Kabul and learned English there," I told him. He then asked me if I had come to the United States alone. I told him about leaving a big family behind, and the fact that they were all in great danger. I then told him again that I was a dedicated worker and would do well in banking.

"Just give me a chance, Mr. Pounds," I said, as I looked at the nameplate on his desk.

He remained curious and leaned back and forth while smoking his pipe. Then he stood up and said, "I will be back—stay here, young man," as he walked away.

I sat there and observed the bank lobby, gazing at people, occasionally looking outside at the busy traffic as cars and people moved up and down the streets, for a good fifteen minutes. Mr. Pounds came back with a middle-aged women dressed very professionally. He introduced her as Gladys Gustafson and said she was also one of the managers of the bank. I stood up and shook her hand. As she sat down next to me, there was a long pause; I realized they did not know what to do with me at that point, but I was convinced they were somehow willing to help me.

"Do you know what a teller job is, young man?" Gladys asked. I told her that I had not known originally and shared my initial understanding of it and what I had learned about it after calling my friend Ahmad. They both laughed hysterically, especially the woman, who had a very distinguished laugh. It all felt weird but very funny, and provided me with much-needed confidence and comfort.

"Mr. Pounds tells me you have no cash-handling experience, though," Gladys said. I told her that was a challenge, but that I was good with money and could practice. The discussion turned into less of an official interview as they both started asking questions about my travel and time away from home during the last couple of years. I told them how miserable, lonely, and depressing refugee conditions in Germany were, and said I wanted to build a career and ultimately rescue my family. Gladys then started to tell me about her own background, and the fact that she had come from Germany.

"You better be careful talking about Germans, young man!" she joked, as she continued to laugh. I told her politely that I did not mean anything bad and actually was grateful for the opportunity to be accepted as a refugee a couple years back, but that it was the waste of talent and time for millions of refugees like me, who could have actually gained some work experience instead of being idle for so long, that had bothered me.

"Where do you see yourself in five years, Attaullah?" the manager eventually asked me.

I first told him that they could call me Atta, then said, without any hesitation, "At your desk."

He immediately turned toward Gladys, and I thought this was the end of my time there. I knew I had made a big mistake, and that I should have expressed my future and progress differently. I honestly thought I had blown my employment chances there at American Savings and Loan.

They both left for a few minutes. When they returned together, they instructed me to fill out an application and hand it over to their personnel representative, Mrs. Louis, downstairs. "She knows you are coming," Mr. Pounds said, "so just take the elevator down, and her office is right next door." He shook my hand.

"Welcome to America," Gladys said, and she extended her hand as well. I shook it and thanked her for the opportunity. She told me to fill out the application at the desk, and to just ask her if I had any questions.

*Wow!* I told myself. *I don't think it is a good idea to fill out the application myself.* I thought I should ask for help the first time I filled out a job application outside of Afghanistan, because I knew I must be careful to not make too many mistakes, but I also realized I was being granted a great opportunity and did not want to lose it. I thought of my friend Homayoun, who was working only a few blocks away at the St. Francis Hotel and decided I could call or see him if I needed help.

I struggled to fill out the application completely, so when I went to Mrs. Louis's office, I told her I had a few questions and asked if it was okay to turn in the application the next day. She was very professional and kind and said that it was fine. I then came back to thank Mr. Pounds and Mrs. Gustafson, and tell them that I would turn in the application the next day. Mr. Pounds said I should not hesitate, as they had several candidates for the job, and I assured him I would turn in it as soon as the bank doors opened the next morning.

I called Ahmad and told him what had happened, but he still could not stop laughing and making fun of me because of the teller story. I asked what was so funny about all this. He said, "Did you change your accent?" I told him how rude he was, that I would never do such a thing, and that both managers actually liked my accent. But he was very happy for me and promised to help me finish filling out the application properly that evening and show me how to dress properly for a bank job. I told him I had a suit but no ties, but Homayoun promised to give me a couple until I was able to buy some on my own. It was a very happy time; I wanted to stop looking for a job that day, but I reminded myself not to get too excited and that I was only turning in an application for now.

I went to the city early the next day and stood outside the bank doors. I arrived at the bank about half an hour early and told the security guard that I was turning in an application. He told me the bank would not open until nine, but said I could take a seat in the lobby. Mr. Pounds saw me waiting there as he let in the arriving employees and he let me inside the bank, where I realized they were about to have a staff meeting. He asked me to wait in the lobby area until the meeting was over; I was gaining confidence by the minute and thought I had made the right move by arriving early and making a good impression.

When he came back, he said, "Okay, I talked about you with Mrs. Gustafson and Mrs. Louis, and they both like you and think we should indeed give you a chance."

"Thank you so much, Mr. Pounds!" I said as I reached to shake his hand. I thought I had been granted a new lease on life in the United States.

"I will do very well and not let you down, Mr. Pounds," I assured him, as he guided me toward the door and told me I would get a call about training and what to do next. I was so overwhelmed that I did not ask about pay, benefits, or anything else, but simply walked out of the building happy and hopeful.

"Can you start training next Monday?" Mrs. Louis asked when she called the next day. I told her that I had no problem with any schedule but was curious if I should ask her about my pay. I was actually very apprehensive and thought it might not be a good idea to ask; that was just the way I had been brought up. But I dared to inquire anyway, and she told me I would be paid a monthly salary of a little more than $700. I did not really know much I would need every month to pay for all my expenses, but I was happy to start, and I had every intention of looking for a second job in order to start helping my big family in Afghanistan.

After the initial excitement of landing a job as an immigrant in America, it was time to face the reality of adjusting and learning about work requirements. After spending a full week in teller training at the bank's Oakland training site, I reported to my branch in San Francisco. I was scared, and had spent the whole week with deep headaches, not so much because of the enormous pressure to learn the basics of banking and money handling as because of the fact that I had not heard from my family for a long time. I had many sleepless nights and had gone to training exhausted and confused every day.

My teller trainers knew that I had much to learn, but they were very kind and graciously provided constant support. Oftentimes I thought I was not made for this job, and that a different line of work might be better suited for me, but I did not want to let anyone down, as I had promised my friends and bank managers repeatedly that I would not.

"Don't worry, I was in a much worse situation than you are." Those were the first words my immediate supervisor, himself an immigrant from Guyana and originally of Indian descent, said to me. He had a great personality and upbeat attitude as he shared his first experiences in America. I told him about my struggles at teller school and thoughts of giving up during our introduction and initial conversation. He laughed and said that was nothing compared with his first job and early years' experiences as an immigrant. I was quite happy, and felt lucky to constantly come in contact with great people during my initial work experience.

I decided to make the best of it, but no matter how much I tried or what I did, my struggles continued for almost a month. Working at the main office, with so much traffic and so much on my mind, I was under a lot of pressure, and it was no easy task to stay motivated. This branch of American Savings and Loan was one of the biggest and busiest offices in the state, with thirty full-time employees, long customer lines, and at least twelve new account desks. I continued to be out of balance and to come home late almost every day because of my consistent errors, due mainly to lack of concentration and focus. I was too worried, paranoid, and distraught over everything to be careful.

I also had a very difficult time communicating with customers and coworkers. I thought I had learned really good English and grammar back home, and I had graduated with great grades, so why was it so difficult to speak to them? I started to call my friends and ask what I was doing wrong and if they had any advice about a new approach, as some customers would show displeasure and at times anger over my questions and comments. I actually told Ahmad that I thought some people here did not speak proper English, and that they were using lots of slang that I did not understand. My roommate just loved moments like these; he started laughing again. "I knew you would have a huge problem with your nasty accent," he said. "Remember, you are supposed to be a storyteller!"

# No One to Nomads

〜〜〜〜〜〜〜〜〜

In August 1982, a family friend who had just arrived from Afghanistan informed me about my family's plan to leave. I asked which country they were fleeing to, but he said, "That is all your brother told me, and he just wanted me to deliver the message."

This was the best news I had gotten since leaving the country, as we still weren't able to send letters or call at that time.

How could my big family move to a secure area? What if they got caught? Would they be safe traveling on foot? What about my mother, at her age? I was once again distraught and had lots of difficulty focusing on my job. After a few weeks, I called some friends in hopes of finding someone in neighboring Pakistan and Iran.

I was able to connect with a close friend in New York, who gave me his brother's phone number in Peshawar, Pakistan. After many attempts, I was able to establish communication with this man's brother and inform him about my family's decision to leave Afghanistan. He was very kind and offered to put the word out and inquire about my brother.

After a couple more weeks, I was awakened around 2:00 AM by the phone ringing. I immediately recognized my older brother's voice as he kept on saying, "Hello, hello."

I could hear him, but he could not hear me, so, after a frustrating few minutes, we had to hang up and wait. A few minutes later, he called again and we finally spoke.

"We arrived a few days ago here in Pakistan but had to wait for Mom to arrive."

"What do you mean?" I asked.

"Well, it is a long story, and I will tell you more later, but we had to split into two groups and decided to send Mom with a family friend [Sakhi] through western Afghanistan and eventually to Peshawar, but we are all here except for two of our sisters." He was referring to our married sister, who had kids, and another sister, who had gone to Europe for her higher education.

"What about my other sister in Hungary?" I asked.

"She can hopefully join the family later," he said.

"Are you in touch with her?" I asked.

"Yes, she is fine, and she can refuse to go to Afghanistan, so let's not worry about her for now," he assured me. "She still has at least two years remaining on her scholarship," he mentioned confidently.

"Ziaullah saved us all," he said repeatedly. I asked him to give Zia a big hug for me and told him that I would take care of things from now on.

"Do you guys have any money?" I asked my brother. He told me they had been able to sell the house after lots of difficulty, and fortunately had enough money to make it to Peshawar; he said to focus on sponsoring the family, and not to worry about sending money to Pakistan.

The family had been moved to my brother-in-law's in Karte Parwan, first, as soon as it became dark one day, splitting into three groups and riding in taxis to avoid being recognized by family and friends. After a couple of nights, they had moved to the home of a trusted friend of our father. Once at the friend's house, they were all instructed, as a precaution, to stay inside for the next twenty-four hours until their departure time after sunset the next day.

The family departed from this friend's house right after dark on May 16, 1982, for the dangerous journey to Pakistan. There was only a couple hours' window between that time and the start of curfew, so the entire family had to be taken out of Kabul within that time frame.

The group, which consisted of males and females of all ages, from one and a half years to over fifty years old, made the decision to send our mother to Pakistan with Sakhi, the same friend who had once deposited all the heavy guns into our well during the neighborhood search. We all considered him to be a true member of our own family. This shorter route would make it easier for my mother, as she would not have to travel by foot during the long and grueling journey.

Many family members would leave for this big journey with only one pair of clothes on and very minimal extra clothing. They were expected to look like ordinary villagers, and to be seen as people of rural areas during travel from the capital to their destination, so they were forced to leave everything behind, as it was not even safe to take items like family photo albums or other valuables with them. Family members would first be expected to travel within small groups, until they were out of the immediate capital area, and then they would join other traveling groups beyond Logar province (located southeast of Kabul) and on toward the mountains.

As they got ready to head toward the high mountain area, a young man on a black horse rushed to inform them about the fact that the area ahead had been occupied by Afghan and Russian army members for twenty-four hours. The man had mentioned that the occupation of this particular mountain was rare, but apparently the news of this group's escape had leaked, and the army had arrived to capture them.

At that point a couple of people from Shaiwaki, who were with them to guide them up to the mountain, decided to divide them into two groups and take them back to houses that were considered safe in a village nearby.

Amid a big rush and constant yelling from the commanders, it took them about twenty minutes to arrive back at the village. The men and women of those houses, as in many other rural areas of Afghanistan, were incredibly hospitable and gracious and acted in true Afghan fashion; they had hosted and helped dozens of passing refugee families on their journey.

The hostesses briefed all the women on how to act and what to say in case the army came to search the houses and ask questions. They were told to say that they had come from another village for the engagement of their son, and to act just like village people and not like city slickers. The men in our group were taken inside a room with only a couple of small openings. Apparently, the reason these two houses were chosen for their safety was because of the hidden places within them that could conceal ten people.

About an hour after the group's arrival inside these houses, the Russian troops, along with their Afghan military counterparts, started to arrive to search the village. They searched some homes twice and took hours, but were not able to find any of the men or any sign of anyone planning to leave the country. All women were fortunately covered with veils and had been instructed not to expose their faces unless questioned by a female member of the search group; the younger ones were instructed to simply remain quiet and not engage in any conversations. The traveling men remained inside the walls for over four hours while the women were questioned.

After almost five hours of this horrifying ordeal, the Russian and Afghan army personnel started to pull out of the village. The capture of a single person, especially my brothers and the other men who had remained motionless inside the big hidden mud walls, would have meant on-the-spot shootings and the end of these families. At that point, no one had any clear idea about the situation or the next destination of the searching army. Combined with the fact that the escaping men were completely exhausted after hiding between the walls for hours, they were advised to spend the night and leave the following evening if it was safe. At this point, they still had not heard from the other part of their group, so neither party had any idea if they were safe or had been found by the army.

Fortunately, during the late afternoon, the two groups were united again to prepare for their departure for the mountain once it was dark and safe. Our brother Zia had some of his best fighters along with him, and they had access to communication equipment, as well as human intelligence. Passage through this area and the mountaintop was very important for the family, as this was the most significant point within the government's and Russian army's reach. The farther away the group got, the more difficult it would become for these authorities to capture them. When the family was finally advised that it was safe, they all headed toward the mountain.

A day later—May 17, 1982—the group marched toward the mountain in darkness, with a willing spirit but weak flesh full of fear and anxiety. The courage, confidence, and strength that Ziaullah and his friends provided for the group gave them the confidence to continue, no matter how difficult and risky the rest of the journey would be.

With a full moon overhead, they reached the top of the first mountain. Then it was time for the group to take one last look at Kabul, which seemed bright—not only because of the city lights, but because of the continuous military surveillance that illuminated many parts of the capital. Their tears of sadness gave way to the need to keep up their momentum.

As they started their descent from the high mountain and were just about a mile below the top, one member of the group, who was walking ahead of everyone, started screaming to stop and not take another step. He called for my brother Zia and another man, and instructed the rest to simply wait until the situation was assessed. My brother Zia and his friend turned on large flashlights to reveal the bodies of several young and middle-aged men on the ground, floating in blood. It was obvious these men had been murdered just recently by Russian and government troops. The members of the group all wept in shock, but they were not able to identify any of the dead, so they were asked to move on while a fighter was sent back to inform the villagers, who could properly bury the bodies.

Once they were down the mountain, the group arrived at a small village ahead of them and were happy for a chance to rest. People of this village, too, were extremely gracious—and, to the group's surprise, they were expecting my brother and the other travelers. He had made previous arrangements with the villagers through trusted men and members of his original resistance groups in this area. They were welcomed to a big lunch with typical Afghan hospitality.

The refugees truly enjoyed the company of the very courageous women and men of this village. However, the short celebration and happiness ended as it became evident that the dead men seen at the bottom of the mountain were indeed sons and husbands of these villagers, who had not yet been notified. It was heartbreaking to find out that the men were these villagers' family members; they had been on their way to Kabul the night before to shop for their food supplies for the upcoming hot summer.

The people of this village asked if the group had crossed paths with their sons and husbands on the mountain. Sadly, none of them was in a position to say anything without instructions from my brother Zia, who eventually gathered the elders of the village to inform them about the murder of their loved ones and whereabouts of their bodies. In the meantime, the refugees found out through my brother's informants that the Russian army had gone back to the mountains and all villages in search of my family and the rest of the group.

As the villagers went to look for the dead and collect their bodies, the group was instructed to leave immediately amid the uncertainty and ongoing danger of Russian assault and pursuit. My family left the village with tremendous disappointment and sorrow, knowing that those sons and husbands had lost their precious lives, but they also felt extremely lucky to be alive.

They then spent the entire night walking, taking only five- to ten-minute breaks, until they reached an abandoned village that had been mostly destroyed, obviously as the result of bombing. Despite the destruction of these homes, the scenery was breathtaking, with clear and delicious water flowing through creeks and streams surrounded by greenery and big trees topped with gorgeous hills, paving the way for a spectacular sunrise.

They ate their prepared meals and finally slept, as the men took turns guarding the group. With nothing solid to sleep on, everyone had to find grass or leaves just to get some rest, as they were all exhausted after walking for miles and miles.

The next morning, May 19, the group continued their walk at around five in the morning, traveling through several mountains, until they reached the tents of some nomads *(kochi)*. The *kochi* were known for their exceptional hospitality and graciousness. They welcomed everyone unconditionally, and offering their tents to the group while they themselves decided to sleep in the cold. They even offered to take their younger kids outside with them. The group's stay with the nomads lifted everyone's spirits, reminded them not to get discouraged at this critical time, and provided much motivation and courage to appreciate life and continue on to their destination and fate.

As my family talked about the *kochi's* amazing spirit, sense of optimism, and consistent smiles, one of my sisters said it was like one of those "aha" moments when you put yourself in these nomads' shoes and imagine what it would feel like to be constantly on the move, without having your own dwelling. The experience taught the group to appreciate life without material possessions, and that there is indeed a home for everyone under the skies. Another sister mentioned that she truly no longer cared or thought about all the belongings our family had left behind after spending time with the *kochi*.

The caravan of fifty men and women spent the next five days traveling toward Pakistan in similar situations, whether they spent the night with other nomads, in the remains of destroyed homes in villages, or in structures in the middle of the jungle. During this journey they had many memorable moments that made them laugh and cry, and which gave everyone tremendous strength, combined with sorrow, as they got farther away from their homeland.

In another great Pashtun city, Paktia, a donkey carrying one of my sisters decided to take a different route, going through a village crowded with alleys. No one in the group, nor my sister herself, noticed this separation at first. After realizing that she was following the wrong crowd, my sister knew it was too dangerous to call for help, so she just waited to see where the donkey would take her and if anyone would come for her. The donkey went through small passages and reached a huge patch of green grass, where she met a group of about ten men, who stood in her way and started to approach her.

Only about ten feet away from the approaching men came the sound of four galloping horses, rushing toward my sister and causing the approaching men to stop, change course, and walk away in a different direction. It was Zia and his friends, riding their horses with amazing speed and determination to find and rescue my sister. Extremely angry and nervous, Zia jumped down from his horse to hug my sister, who was terrified. Expecting to be scolded, she instead found herself in our brother's arms, surrounded by warmth and words of comfort. Little did she know, the area was one of the most dangerous crossing points and centers for the sale of ammunition, as well as a safe haven for drug smugglers and human traffickers.

On May 23, the refugees finally reached Peshawar, the closest Pakistani city to the Afghan border, situated in a large valley near the end of the Khyber Pass.

The group went to a hotel while awaiting my mother's arrival. Despite having achieved this big milestone of rescuing the majority of my family, they wondered about her whereabouts. They had actually expected her and Sakhi to arrive earlier, due to their expected journey by car, but there was no guarantee in light of all the fighting, constant bombing, and closure of roads throughout the country. With no phone access, they just had to rely on word of mouth and messages through other refugee groups. My family knew only that our mom had left through the west because of her access to a car, so they knew she and Sakhi would eventually go through Iran, on the open deserts and roads leading to Iran and Pakistan throughout the southwest regions of Afghanistan. Still, no one's safety could be guaranteed. Some of the resistance groups in the area were notorious for demanding cash from refugees and other travelers. The area was also dangerous because of smuggling activities, but we derived some confidence and comfort from the fact that everyone still treated elderly women with particular respect.

At the hotel, my brothers and friends immediately went out to ask if someone had seen our mother along the way. My brother visited at least ten refugee camps and other areas where people congregated, so as not to miss any opportunities to learn news about our mother.

In the late afternoon on the second day after the group's arrival in Peshawar, a hotel employee rushed to my family's rooms to inform them about our mother's arrival. The entire family rushed downstairs to welcome and embrace her, Sakhi, and accompanying refugees who had become their travel partners along the way—a group that included Dr. Ashraf Ghani, who eventually became an Afghan presidential candidate during the 2010 elections, and his family.

# The Ford Maverick and
# My Family's Arrival

AFTER MY INITIAL STRUGGLES and lack of focus at work, as well as many sleepless nights, due to my personal frustration about my family's rescue plans, I realized that I could not jeopardize my job and needed to actually improve my performance if I was to bring my big family to America. So I started to focus on working extra hard and attending various banking, management, and leadership classes. Within months I was promoted to new accounts, and, shortly thereafter, to operations officer of my branch.

After earning these promotions and pay raises, I knew it was time to think about buying my first car. I contacted a family friend, who lived in Concord and bought and fixed up cars for resale, and told him that I needed to get an inexpensive four-door car that would take care of my big family's needs. He suggested a van, but I told him that I could not afford a van now. Within a few weeks, he called me and told me he had found a perfect car, in good condition and big enough to carry at least four to five passengers.

"How much, and what kind of car is it?"

"A nice Ford Maverick," he said. I had no idea what a Maverick was, but I had heard about Ford, so I thanked him and told him that I was just so excited to get my first car in the United States. He had called me on a Tuesday, at a time when I had to work 'til late in the evening and also attend banking classes at night, but I wanted to see the car so badly that I actually skipped a class that week to go get it.

"There it is," my friend said, pointing to a big, ugly orange car parked below his apartment building.

"Why orange? Could you not find another color?" I asked.

He started laughing and told me this was a very strong, classic car. He said, "Don't worry about the color—worry about the engine. I drove it a couple times, and it sounds real good."

I was stunned and no longer happy, as this man was related to my original sponsor in America and, out of respect, I wasn't able to tell him no.

"I may still have to change the color," I told him.

"That is no problem; I know people who can do it very cheaply," he told me convincingly as he walked around the car, showing me the engine and the interior. It all looked okay, except for the color. I knew my friends would have a field day laughing at me.

"So, how much is the price?" I asked

"Eight hundred dollars," he said.

I paid him and drove off feeling subdued. The car moved with good power during the few miles from his house in Concord to Alameda, but I was now concerned about how to show my first car to my friends, so I parked the car on the street and did not let my roommate know about it right away.

I no longer had time to worry about my orange Maverick, however, when I faced the almost impossible task of finding a home big enough to accommodate eleven people. I went to work on it right away by talking to landlords and friends throughout the Alameda area. I was living in Concord, but planned to bring the family closer to bigger cities and an Afghan community in order to lead a successful lives and not fall victim to typical government support. I had observed millions of Afghan refugees becoming dependent on welfare and other government support programs. While I respected the need for support during the early stages of refugees' lives, I knew these programs to be extremely harmful to long-term recipients' social and financial well-being, so I was determined to get my family members on the right track from the beginning.

As their arrival drew closer, I got more and more nervous about finding a place. Although some advised me to give up my search in Alameda and move to smaller communities outside of the Bay Area, I kept at it because of my concerns over lack of jobs and growth elsewhere.

Then my friend Homayoun again came to my rescue! He and his family knew about my family's arrival and were actively searching for a residence for us, and one day he called about a three-bedroom apartment—with a small den and only one bathroom—that he had found in Alameda, about a hundred yards away from his own house. He had spoken to the landlord and informed him about my family situation, and had asked him to talk to me.

Mr. Schroeder was a retired army officer and a Vietnam War veteran who had an amazing knowledge and awareness about Afghanistan and the Soviet invasion, so we spent a good hour talking about that instead of the rental terms.

"Tell me, how many people in the family?" he asked.

I looked him in the eye and hesitantly told him, "Eleven." I told him if he helped me get this place, I would promise to split up my family and look for another place for my brother, his wife, and a couple of my sisters. I told him I knew it sounded crazy, but we would take very good care of his place. I also told him I was running out of time and would appreciate his support. Mr. Schroeder simply remained quiet and did not say anything for a while.

"They have been living inside one house for almost a year in Pakistan as refugees," I told him. "They need help. I will have them work very hard, and maybe we can rent another unit of your apartments right here and stay for a long time."

"This is my own property, and I have worked very hard for it," he told me. "I am actually suffering from an illness and don't need any headaches."

"I guarantee you will not have a problem with them," I told him again.

"The apartment is yours! But I have to collect first and last months' rent, plus a one-thousand-dollar deposit," he said with a smile, while extending his arm to shake my hand.

I was truly happy and grateful. Then it was on to preparation and getting the house ready for the eleven members of my family. The local Lutheran church instructed me to meet with them about all my needs and told me that they would provide a resource guide with a list of places I could go in order to prepare the house for my family's arrival. Within a week, I was busy searching through a long list of discount stores, charity organizations, and even free markets for any household items I could afford.

Because of these low-priced deals, I was becoming more and more encouraged as time went by. I knew we did not have enough space for eleven inside this small three-bedroom apartment—and continued to search for smaller items, such as mattress and blankets, in preparation for a refugee lifestyle—but I was still happy and motivated. Within a few weeks, I got sleeping and other household items ready and delivered for all members of the family. A good friend even donated a TV set while my coworkers at the bank bought a complete set of dishes, for which I was very grateful.

"We are good to go," Qudrat informed me on the phone during a midnight call from Pakistan. "But I have to tell you that Zia will not be coming with us at this time."

"What do you mean?" I asked.

"He is all right," replied my older brother, "but he decided to go back to Afghanistan until he can bring our older sister with him. Now, he is continuing his fight against the Russians. He will join us at a later date."

"But how about the American embassy? Are they okay with his refusal to come along with the family?" I asked.

"Yes, we actually went to the consulate and informed them that Zia wants to stay back for a while to rescue our sister and then come to the United States."

"What did they say?" I asked with curiosity.

"They were very nice and told him he is welcome to join the family whenever he is ready," he assured me.

After much anticipation and waiting, my family was finally coming to America, and I realized we were one of the luckiest families; we had survived, while many large families had lost loved ones during the years of war and chaos. I went to airports in the United States and Germany with friends many times, simply to accompany them as they welcomed their families. I got a fair amount of satisfaction and happiness out of these experiences, which felt like rehearsal for someday welcoming my own family. Now, as the realization of my dream drew near, quite a few friends volunteered to join me at the

San Francisco airport and help drive my family back to Alameda. We also had three Lutheran social services representatives with us who had become great friends and wanted to welcome my big family.

While waiting behind the customs line with these people, I started feeling extremely nervous. I was a little dizzy and could feel my stomach turning. I honestly did not know what my reaction would be when I finally laid eyes on my family members. I had not slept for many nights, so, while their arrival was my biggest pleasure and a dream come true, I was feeling drained. A friend at the airport who realized I was not feeling well took me away for a while to make me eat a sandwich and drink lots of water, but I was still feeling sick as we waited outside customs for well over an hour.

"We made it!" yelled my youngest sister, who was the first to come out and see me.

Within moments I was hugging and holding on to my mother, sisters, brother, and brother's new wife. It was one big party—the three members of the Lutheran church and several other friends clapped, chanting, "Welcome!" It felt like some heroes' welcome for a while as bystanders realized it was a huge family reunion. It was not an easy moment for anyone to miss, as we were all crying. It was without a doubt one of the sweetest memories I have; it will never fade away.

"Wow, it is beautiful here," sighed my youngest sister as we cruised through San Francisco. She kept on looking up and down the sky-scrapers at awe. "So different from Peshawar," she joked.

I told her there was no comparison indeed, while assuring her this was the safest and most beautiful place in the world. "We are very lucky to be here," I told her and my mother. My mother could not stop crying! She was visibly happy, but at times would mention my younger brother's name. We tried to comfort her, and promised to bring him here as well.

"He has always been a smart fighter—he will make it here," we assured her.

"I am very sorry for having such a small place," I told my family as we sat for our first dinner as a group after three years.

"This is wonderful," my brother responded. "You should have been with us in Pakistan. This is great."

"I want you all to be thankful and never forget your past," he told everyone.

"Innocent people are dying like flies, but here we are, safe under one roof, with amazing possibilities," my mother said. "Let's pray together and thank God in memory of your father. I am sure he is happy for all of us."

We all prayed together, which reminded us all of the great, peaceful days when families prayed together a few times during each meal. It felt so good. Everyone looked happy and energized to start the next journey of life in America!

"Let's go to work!" I told my entire family right after dinner. I gathered them in our living room to share my plans for us. "We are all going to work and succeed in America," I told them right off the bat. "I have seen it all, from Germany to here. We must get to work in order to be successful, or you will become a victim, like millions of others who rely on government support and sit idle. That is no way to make a living and no way to succeed here.

"I don't want anyone except for Mom to be on welfare for more than ninety days to six months max," I continued, warning them of dire consequences and failure if we did nothing. I was quite determined to put them all in various schools and colleges. I had done lots of research before their arrival, and was quite comfortable with the process of applying for financial aid, registration, and entry into nursing schools, etc. I told my brother he would make an excellent airplane mechanic in the States, since he had graduated from an aeronautics school in Kabul; I was similarly confident that the rest of my siblings would be successful as well.

I also described my lazy and wasted year and a half in Germany, without work or any opportunity to contribute and serve as a productive member of a new society, while being forced to depend on government aid. I explained that refugees in Germany did not have a choice, but being in the United States provided great opportunities for education and work and it was up to them to go as far as they wanted to.

"We want to be successful and have no plan to stay home," my older sister said. "No way are we going to stay on government support. Let's get to work tomorrow—I am ready!"

I was happy to see her determination, but had to be realistic about the fact that my family had to rely on welfare support for a little while. Education first!

After my family members applied for Social Security and identification cards, I thought it was important for all of them except my mother to enroll in English or vocational training classes. We agreed as a family that learning English was our number-one need and responsibility. We needed to be able to speak, write, and fully participate as active members of this new society, and prove that we had the ability to earn a living. While odd, it felt like being back in school; the entire household buzzed with homework, so the small apartment started to sound and look like a dorm.

"I like you guys to eat together," were my mother's determined words one day, after seeing many of us eat at different times in between attending various schools and language classes.

"But, Mother, we are no longer in Afghanistan. Look at every-one's school and work schedules. How can we all eat at the same time?" someone asked. We knew she was not happy with the answer, but also that she was starting to accept the fact that she was no longer in Afghanistan and had to adjust to being confined in an apartment with no yard.

# A Sister Lost in Europe

AFTER THE FAMILY HAD SETTLED, and with the majority of us busy with school and part-time jobs, it was time to focus on locating my sister Shuky, who was missing in Europe. She was a very determined and proud Afghan girl, so we hoped she would somehow be safe and secure and would surround herself with the right crowd—but with the turmoil and uncertainty surrounding refugees, it was hard not to worry about her getting out of Hungary, where she had gone for her advanced education. As part of the family plan to rescue as many members from Afghanistan as possible after the Russian invasion, Shuky had obtained a scholarship through work and had left for Hungary in August 1981.

With human trafficking rampant at the time, primarily in Eastern European countries, we were extremely concerned about Shuky, as traffickers smuggled thousands of refugees from Afghanistan and various former Soviet Union states to western Europe. We knew that the majority of these refugees were single men or families with children, as no single woman could travel or escape without a family companion, and that my sister was a very smart and respected student among the Afghan community within Hungary and would not venture to leave without proper support and guidance. However, it was time for us to act, as we did not want to take the chance of waiting until the end of her studies came and she faced the possibility of being sent back to Afghanistan.

Planning an escape from Hungary or from any other country that was a communist ally of the Soviet Union was extremely difficult, as most students were considered committed members of the Communist Party, with government ties; all Afghan escapees had to strategize secretly and be extremely careful about their communication with the outside world. Shuky had warned us in one of her letters that our written correspondence might even be reviewed by authorities in Hungary. Even though we tried hard to use extra caution in our writing, we found it less risky to communicate by phone. We started our discussions at an advantage, since she asked to speak in Pashto rather than Farsi, as she felt more comfortable doing so. Both our parents had come from Pashtun families, so speaking both languages for all members of the family was normal.

After months of research and talking to friends and families within European communities, we found that Shuky had officially started her attempt to escape, with a plan to go through Yugoslavia en route to Switzerland or Austria as a refugee.

In January 1983, my sister, along with another female friend, traveled by train through Yugoslavia as part of a student vacation plan in an attempt to seek political asylum in either Switzerland or Austria. They were able to travel through Yugoslavia without much difficulty, but Swiss authorities refused to grant them asylum, insisting that she must know another Afghan national within Switzerland. The first destination of most refugees traveling alone was not a country where they had relatives waiting for them, we thought. So Shuky had to go back to Yugoslavia, where it felt okay to stay, as a couple of her former classmates lived in Belgrade. She was determined to not return to Hungary, however.

She was able to finally call us from Belgrade after her disappointing return from Switzerland. I then advised her to try Austria, as did her friends in Belgrade. This was a trick that worked most of the time, as travelers who stopped first at a different destination than their final one would be less subject to questioning. As a family, we felt as if our hands were tied; despite having close friends in Germany and some other Western European countries, we knew we would somehow lose contact with Shuky during her travel. It was very dangerous and unnerving, as some refugees would end up being sent back to their own countries, while other suspected refugees would be subject to constant harassment, tailgating, etc.

After three days in Belgrade, Shuky was able to buy a train ticket to Austria. She made her way to Vienna, where she asked for political asylum upon arrival.

"She is in Austria," were the first words out of my friend Wahid's mouth when he called me from New York.

"Who told you this?" I asked him right away.

He informed me that a member of his family, who had just made it to New York from Austria, had met my sister before his departure. I had previously given my sister Wahid's number in New York in case she was unable to reach anyone in our family, and that was how she had delivered the message.

"She is in a refugee camp along with several other Afghans and should be calling you soon," Wahid indicated.

I immediately informed the entire family and started to work with Lutheran social services to start her U.S. immigration application to join us.

A few hours after receiving the news from New York, I received the call we had been anxiously waiting for.

"I am safe and okay," Shuky stated. Though she was crying hard and was exhausted, she sounded very happy to have made it safely out of the Eastern European bloc, and informed us that she was in very good company in Austria, with several Afghan families.

In the meantime, as the Russian occupation of Afghanistan continued and my brother Zia became more and more involved in his prominent role as a resistance fighter, we decided to do whatever we could to support him, with the understanding that he was staying away from the nasty arms and ammunition dealings and abuse of money by various fighting factions. We knew the majority of the true freedom fighters sacrificed their blood and time without receiving any monetary rewards, so we were committed to providing Zia with financial backing as he continued his fight for the freedom of our beloved country.

"Just send me some money for clothes," he said during one of his phone calls.

"How about arms and weapons? Those things cost a lot," I replied.

"We have plenty," he said. "There are more than enough weapons to go around."

He repeated that he needed money mainly for clothing. Even food was not as high a priority, as fighters ate together and oftentimes were fed well as guests of villagers. "We eat once or twice a day," Zia told us. "We eat bread with yogurt, and occasionally with cheese and butter in the morning, and we drink plenty of milk, so not only does it taste good, but we are okay and energized," he explained, trying to reassure us. "I just need to buy clothes for winter, when it gets really cold."

We continued to send as much money as we could on a monthly basis.

ᏚᎧᏚᎧᏚᎧᏚᎧ

At the time of my family's departure, the American consulate in Islamabad, Pakistan, had been kind enough to agree to postpone Zia's trip to America until whenever he was ready. After a couple years in the United States, we were notified about my brother's open file by the Lutheran social services office in San Francisco and asked whether he was still interested in joining the family.

After receiving this notice, I tried to get hold of Zia. I was able to reach a close friend of his in Pakistan and told him to have my brother call us immediately. Within a week, I spoke with Zia on the phone and delivered the news that his open visa would expire within the next three months and that he had to come to the United States now.

"Can I come back to Pakistan from America?" was the first thing he asked.

"Yes." I told him that he should be able to go back, but not until after at least a year. "You can't lose this opportunity, or you may never be able to come to the U.S.," I said.

"I am in the midst of this big war against Russia," he answered, but not with anger.

I told him we all understood and supported his effort, but said maybe this was a good opportunity to take a little time off and spend time with his family. "Seems like the Russians will be there for a long time," I said.

"But we don't want them to be in our country for too long," he replied. "They are weak and very vulnerable."

I told him we did not have a choice, as the U.S. consulate could not hold the visa open for too much longer; I said the family missed him too much, that he would enjoy his visit, and that he was welcome to return to Pakistan someday.

"Our mother and sisters are worried to death," I also told him. I gave him a week to make his decision; I knew he wasn't happy about my requests, but I did not want him to miss out on his chance to join his family after spending years in a war zone.

"I will only do this for my family," Zia said, his voice breaking, when he called a few days after. I realized he was very emotional about this big decision, and that he would have a very difficult time telling his friends and fellow fighters at this critical stage of their mission, but I told him it was our mother's wish for him to come to the United States.

Within a month, my brother arrived in America. While our family, especially my mother, was extremely happy, Zia had a very tough time adjusting to his new life. He was tired and very frustrated by Afghanistan's occupation, talking constantly about his mission, and everything looked and sounded foreign to him. Just imagine coming fresh from the mountains and a war zone to the luxury of life in America. Still, a few of his school friends and former soccer teammates had made to the United States, and we knew they were happy to see him. Many of them told us about the amazing sacrifices he had made over the years and confirmed that it was time for him to take a break.

Within a couple months, Zia's friends had arranged to get him a job as a cab driver at Oakland Airport, and he became a little happier as he learned the logistics and his way around the area, despite his very limited English. While he struggled for a while, he was able to overcome the obvious challenges of adjusting to life and work in America rather easily, as he was surrounded by friends. Within months, he seemed to do just fine, driving his cab and saving a little money to help his fellow fighters in Afghanistan.

In the meantime, in order to further encourage him to stay in America, my mother was trying to persuade him to get married; but Zia told us that he would never marry anyone in the United States, and would rather go back to Afghanistan and get married there. My mother told him that she would love to see him bring his wife back to the United States.

After one year, Zia decided to go back to Pakistan, where he joined his fellow fighters and continued his quest to get Russians out of Afghanistan. We were informed that Zia had spent only a couple of nights in Peshawar before he left to take part in one of the biggest operations to date against the Russian army. The mujahideen fighters' plan was to launch a massive ambush against Russian troops in the southern part of Afghanistan. During the three-day operation, at least a thousand mujahideen lost their lives, though they caused huge casualties among the Russian and Afghan armies as well.

In this ambush, two young brothers of Zia's closest friend died on the battlefield within an hour of each other, when rockets launched from inside the army garrison blew them up only a few feet away from Zia and his friend. As Zia and his best friend gathered their body parts, they encountered quite a few other fighters who had sustained extensive injuries, though Zia was unharmed. This incident was not only devastating for my brother and his friend, but in many ways made them rethink their plans so that they could be more careful and avoid too much risk.

When I spoke with Zia for the first time after the bombings, he said that he had been deeply impacted, and that he was thinking about taking a break and actually listening to our mother and family about getting married and starting a family. This was good news, as we thought this commitment would bring him closer to us.

However, we knew that we could not convince him to get married in the United States, so we encouraged him to find someone in Afghanistan and eventually bring her to America and raise his family here.

# Traditional Marriage

I HAD MADE A COMMITMENT to myself to not get married until every member of my family was safe and secure, so by the time I thought it was time to start my own family, I had no idea that my family had already begun searching for a wife for me. My mother and sister-in-law had been looking into the possibility of connecting with a former coworker of my brother and sister-in-law, a woman who also lived Alameda, and introducing me to her younger sister, Adiba, who had recently arrived in Pakistan as a refugee.

"We found you a beautiful girl!" my mother told me one day in 1986.

"How come no one has told me anything about it?" I asked.

"Well, we wanted to find the right one for you first," she explained with a broad smile.

"But, Mother, things are different in America. I hope she lives somewhere here," I responded politely.

"Well, she is not here now, but she will be here soon. We have been thinking about you and her since we arrived here," my mother said.

"So, you are talking about someone outside the U.S.?" I asked.

"Yes," she said, with an even broader smile. "Your brother's wife has been talking to her friend about it for quite some time. Her friend's younger sister is beautiful and is now in Pakistan, waiting to come to America within a few months."

"But, Mother, I can't marry someone who is not here—I have no idea who she is!" I protested, though I knew had to be careful about my tone and manner when I spoke to my mother.

"She is truly a beautiful girl and from a nice family; we have done our research," she said, with a genuine sense of optimism and happiness. "Your sister-in-law has pictures of her, but we wanted to wait to tell you first."

I realized my mother and family had been talking about this with my sister-in-law, who worked for the same bank I did, for months. This was quite common, as Afghan families with young girls talk about and plan for their daughters' future well in advance. My sister-in-law told me later that other interested families had inquired about Adiba and actually had pressured her family to respond even while she was still in Pakistan, awaiting her departure to the United States.

I became more interested and curious as I started to ask more questions about her. I asked to see her picture.

"She is pretty and tall," my sister-in-law commented, as she showed me the photo. I was careful to be polite and respectful as I looked.

"She is the one," my sister-in-law said. "God willing, she is probably your fate, but we have to talk more with her sister, and we must hurry so that her family does not say yes to someone else in Pakistan. We can't lose her."

"We honestly believe she is your type," she said, and she continued to stress the importance of acting now.

"Well, tell them we are interested, and also tell them not to make any promises to any other family and not to jeopardize their travel to America," I said. "She may never make it here if she gets engaged to someone there in Pakistan." Despite my growing interest in this girl, I could not imagine why her or other young girls were being rushed to marry. In light of all the chaotic refugee conditions, it just did not make any sense.

"Okay, I need to meet with her sister and tell her you like her, too," my sister-in-law told me.

"Thanks, but please tell her to not rush things, and to just let her sister come here first," I told her. I was genuinely concerned about making any commitment, and thought I would not want any of my sisters to make a hasty decision that would potentially ruin their future.

After leaving Afghanistan and living in Western society, I had a much greater admiration for and understanding of the process of getting married and starting a family with an open mind. On the other hand, I had great respect for the traditional, arranged marriages that have been exercised in my culture for centuries with amazing success and with far better results than Western society's. Above all, I wanted to be practical and realistic about my modern environment. I knew that even within Afghanistan and other Asian cultures, despite the practice of traditional arranged marriages, more and more educated young women and men had been able to meet and get to know their future spouses before their wedding.

Within a couple weeks, we learned that Adiba's family's visa had been issued and they would be arriving in the United States within a month. While this was very good news, it was mixed with a big sense of responsibility and genuine anxiety. We all had a pretty good idea about refugee status and how tempting it might be for someone who simply wished to make it to a safe land like America to agree to marry someone there without thinking beyond the immediate advantages. In light of this, I shared my mother's guilt about putting so much pressure on her family—but I also realized we had no choice, as Adiba was already being pursued by other families.

We found out later that her family had been threatened and harassed many times by mujahideen groups targeting families with adult girls for marriage. Many refugees would actually keep their travel plans secret to avoid such harassment and even the risk of being taken as hostages because of their plans to go to the U.S. or Europe. Adiba's family had moved away from Peshawar to avoid having to deal with political and warring-faction pressures, but was having a very difficult time denying families' demands for marriage, so they were still struggling constantly.

In the United States, the Afghan community was growing rapidly, but there seemed to be a big gap between the numbers of Afghan men and women. Many single men had been able to make their way out of Afghanistan, so there was a huge demand for Afghan girls, as many of these men had not yet acclimated to American life and the majority were not ready to commit to non-Afghan marriages. Single men and their families wanted to stay informed about new relationships and refugee arrivals in hopes of making connections and finding female partners.

With this in mind, my family started to discuss how to approach the situation once Adiba's family arrived. Because of their close relationship with Adiba's sister and her sister's husband, my sister-in-law and brother decided to go and welcome the family at the airport. This was an exciting but anxious time for everyone in my big family, because of their desire to see me get married soon.

Some of my sisters even talked about going to the airport to welcome the family as well, but we convinced them to give up on that idea and that a couple of our family members would be sufficient.

"They don't even know us—let's not scare them right away," I told my sisters. A couple of them seemed really disappointed about not being able to go to the airport to welcome their potential future sister-in-law. The fact that they were acting like she already belonged to our family gave me a funny feeling of confidence and enthusiasm. Everyone seemed to be sure about what was about to transpire, despite my clear warnings about the fact that I had to meet the girl and be able to get to know her before any decisions could be made; they all continued to act as if they had made up my mind for me.

"Wow, she is very pretty," my sister-in-law told us, after coming back from the airport. She told me that the family seemed very nice and a good fit for ours. But she quickly mentioned that she had become aware of some interest in Adiba from another man and family in Alameda. She sounded a little concerned, and thought we needed to approach them right away. By this time my family had invested so much interest and optimism in Adiba that they had no plans to allow someone else to step in ahead of us.

"This is crazy." I told them how badly I felt. "I have lived away from Afghanistan for a few years now, and I understand how people think and feel about their children. Let's not rush this thing," I insisted.

"But you are going to lose a great opportunity, son," my mother said firmly.

"Well, if this is our fate, then it will happen, but it seems like we are now competing with someone else for a wife," I insisted.

"Don't tell me you don't believe in our traditions anymore," she responded angrily.

"No, Mother, I love our traditions and cannot see myself getting married to anyone other than an Afghan girl, but I want us to be realistic," I told her.

"Okay, you don't have to worry—we know what to do," she said with authority.

Within days I was informed that my mom, my brother and his wife, and one of my sisters were going to Adiba's family's home to say hello. There was nothing wrong with this decision, as traditionally Afghans would go to see new visitors and offer their support, but in this case I was confident both families knew exactly what was transpiring—and in reality, both sides seemed to be welcoming the early exchanges. By then my sister-in-law had done some more research and found out more about the very serious interest of a family who happened to live within the same apartment unit as my future potential wife, so there was now a real sense of urgency to build a relationship with her family before they did.

A group of four from my family went to see them and officially welcomed them to America by inviting them for a dinner, which was a traditional gesture.

"I have a good idea," my sister-in-law mentioned, after coming home. "Why not invite them to the engagement party?" she said. One of my sisters' engagement parties was within a few weeks, so it made a lot of sense.

"I think that is a great idea," I answered, as everyone laughed.

"You will be able to see Adiba, too, and see if you really like her," one of my sisters added.

"They already know we like her, so let's work on building relationships and having their entire family at the engagement party," mentioned another sister.

"You guys have not mentioned if she is interested in me," I pointed out.

"We all act like she has already agreed to a marriage here," said my mother.

"I want to be able to have a say about my future husband, so you guys need to calm down a little," my sister chimed in.

"I honestly think inviting them to the engagement party is a very good idea," I mentioned again.

I had been hearing nothing but good things, but thought it would be good to see my family take a slightly more realistic approach by allowing Adiba and me to get to know each other, so it was very good news that we could invite her and her family to the party. These developments and all the talk about our future had become overwhelming and intimidating. This family was fresh off the boat in the United States, and now that I was suddenly finding myself in competition for a wife, just as if I were still inside Afghanistan, I knew I had to be extra careful and conduct myself with perfect, gentlemanly behavior.

My sister's engagement party, to be held at a nice Oakland-area hall, was shaping up to be an even more important event now, as it represented not only the joy of a first family engagement in America but also the prospect of meeting my future spouse.

ﻼﻼﻼﻼ

"They're here!" called my youngest sister, as she ran toward me to inform me of Adiba and her family's arrival at the hall.

"I will introduce myself later—you go," I told her, as I turned away from her. "I would rather go to their table and be introduced to them by someone later."

I knew my sister was not very happy with my behavior, as I just kept on walking down the hallway, but I was extremely nervous and did not want to appear aggressive; I simply wanted to buy time. I decided to get out of the building, and I went for a short walk outside. After a few minutes, I went behind the windows in hopes of looking inside the hall in order to see my future bride. I glanced at her through the glass from about a hundred yards away, and there she was—she looked exactly as I had envisioned.

At that point, I decided to go inside and introduce myself to the table. After a short introduction, we politely exchanged greetings with all members of her family and left. I really liked her, but once again asked my sister-in-law if the family would agree for me to meet with her on my own. She told me right away that this was not possible, because Adiba's mother and brother would not agree to such a meeting, so I knew this evening would the only opportunity for me to make up my mind before my family made a formal proposal. This was a unique situation, since men and women outside Afghanistan—and even educated ones inside the country—were being granted more and more opportunities to meet their spouses in advance; but given the other suitor and his family's persistence, we knew we had to act in order not to lose this big opportunity for me to get married.

Within a week my mother, my brother, and his wife went to Adiba's home for the initial proposal. The first unofficial proposal visit is traditionally made by an elder of the family, followed by multiple additional visits and requests in order to convince the bride's family. My family and I were ready to make as many as visits as possible, but my mom and sister-in-law informed us that Adiba's mother was not happy to let her daughter go away so soon. She had told my mother during her first visit to not rush them, as they had barely landed here after a long struggle as refugees. My mother had told them that we would honor their request, if it weren't for the persistence of this other family—that we did not want to wait too long and miss our chance. My family had told them everything about me and my accomplishments, so we knew we had obtained their trust and confidence in my qualifications as a husband now, despite their recent arrival and tough conditions.

"You never know about the future, though," my mother told us. "They could change their minds later."

ᘓᕽᘓᕽᘓᕽ

"They have agreed!" were the first words out of my sister's mouth when she called me at work to tell me Adiba's mother had called and agreed to officially give their okay to our family. I did not know what to say.

"Aren't you happy?" my sister asked.

"Of course I am—it just feels so different and awkward," I told her. Though I was tens of thousands of miles away, I suddenly felt like I was right back in Kabul, getting married according to old-fashioned Afghan tradition.

I decided to inform my manager and coworkers as soon as possible, so I announced the decision to everyone the next day. I loved my coworkers and had grown very close to them—especially my manager, Mr. Pounds, who was like a real father to me and many workers—so it felt quite natural to share the good news with them as I would with members of my own family.

With a few Afghan families and friends at that time in the Bay Area, we held a very warm and happy family party in Alameda in September 1986. In the meantime, I was successfully accepted to join my bank's management training program, which led to my promotion to my first manager's position. So we remained engaged in order

205

to get ready for a big wedding while Adiba attended language and advanced college classes in Alameda.

In September 1987, we got married in Berkeley in a very traditional setting, in the presence of all my coworkers and many friends and family members. At the wedding, we were surprised with a huge honeymoon gift from my coworkers: a full week's paid vacation in Hawaii.

# Afghanistan Deserted

$\text{\textcyrillic{ʕ}ɾ\text{ʕ}ɾ\text{ʕ}ɾ\text{ʕ}ɾ}$

After years of struggle and mounting casualties in their fight to hold on to Afghanistan, the Russian army was defeated and forced to leave in February 1989. But in spite of continuing pressure from the well-armed mujahideen, the Russian-installed government of Najibullah remained in power until April 1992, when he ultimately sought refuge at the United Nations' office in Kabul as mujahideen forces closed in on the city.

Yes, the mighty Soviet Union had crumbled and fallen to its knees. The cost of its decade-long war was in the billions of dollars. With much doubt about its strength and resources, combined with this big psychological defeat, the Soviet government would never be the same again—and yes, the Afghans had everything to do with the collapse of the Soviet Union and the end of its dream to open a path to a warm-water port on the Indian Ocean.

This long and bloody Afghan war against the invading Russian army had denied the Soviets' own people money they badly needed to better their living conditions. More than $4 billion dollars each year went toward sustaining the Soviet-installed Kabul government; other costs of running the war over ten years were estimated to be thirty times that amount. A world superpower was unable to defeat a disorganized and tattered but determined army of mujahideen standing in their way.

The Russian defeat, and the ultimate withdrawal of their forces from Afghanistan was the most welcome news for Afghans around the world. I remember celebrating at a huge gathering of Afghans in a friend's house in Alameda. Every detail of the Russians' departure seemed to provide a spark and a sense of optimism to every Afghan who hoped to someday return to their homeland, especially in light of statements from the United Nations indicating its agreement to stay engaged.

Still, how was it possible for the UN to guarantee the safety of millions of people under a very insecure and incompetent Russian-installed government? Afghanistan had become a devastated and deserted state by the late 1980s, with at least two million casualties, some five million refugees around the world, and a population torn between supporting their local freedom fighters and their inability to turn their backs on local government. Within ten years, hundreds of thousands of young Afghans had become members of the ruling Communist Party by force, heavy recruitment, or simple intimidation.

As the Russian bear was going home, the West intended to make it as painful as possible. The Russians were well aware that the United States viewed the Soviet-Afghan war as an opportunity to exact revenge for its own humiliation in Vietnam. For years the United States and a few European nations in the Cold War era had been supplying the mujahideen with hundreds of millions of dollars in weapons and aid. By 1984, the United States was authorizing military supplies to mujahideen of nearly $250 million per month. Then it increased the prize even further by authorizing the supply of over one thousand Stinger surface-to-air missiles and training the mujahideen to use them.

Not only was the Soviet regime's initial justification for its invasion—to help stabilize an unpopular government and political system in Afghanistan—no longer a valid claim, but its defeat actually started to motivate several other neighboring republics to think of their own independence.

The various Afghan factions who fought Russia during its military occupation occasionally had run-ins with each other, but had remained largely united against the Russian army. They had also established various territories of control around the country while benefiting from direct support from the United States and other Western countries, as well as Arab nations. With Afghans inside and outside of Afghanistan celebrating the Russians' defeat, it was now time to turn attention to the aftermath of the Russian withdrawal and the fate of the weak Afghan government.

As the citizens' displeasure spread throughout Afghanistan and various external resistance groups drew strength from broad financial and military support, the government of Afghanistan—led by Dr. Najibullah, the fourth government leader to have been handpicked by the Soviets—weakened day by day, until it ultimately collapsed in 1992. Afterward, the leaders of the external parties and those inside Afghanistan jointly created an interim government that was officially recognized by the United Nations as the Islamic State of Afghanistan.

With the fall of the Najibullah government, the seven-party alliance of the Islamic groups based in Pakistan tried to consolidate its achievement by announcing plans to set up an interim Afghan government charged with paving the way for elections. The alliance moved to affirm its domination of Afghanistan, but its efforts to establish the IAG in Kabul failed when, within ten days of Najibullah's departure from office, two well-armed forces of Islamic resistance groups clashed for control of the capital.

Continued fighting between warring militias halted further progress. Before the end of the year, upwards of a million Afghans had fled the city. Deep differences among the leadership, exacerbated by decades of bad blood, distrust, and personal enmity, prevented any further progress toward creating a genuine interim government capable of honoring the 1992 pledge to write a constitution, organize elections, and create a new Afghan polity. Despite UN attempts to broker peace and bring the warring groups into a coalition government, Afghanistan remained at war.

By the summer of 1994, the Afghan people were victimized once again as warring factions brought the economy to a halt. On the main highway leading to the eastern province of Kandahar, a convoy owned by influential Pakistani businessmen was stopped by bandits demanding money. The businessmen pleaded for support from the Pakistani government, which responded by encouraging Afghan students from the fundamentalist religious schools on the Pakistan-Afghan border to intervene. The students freed the convoy and went on to capture Kandahar, Afghanistan's second-largest city.

Also in July 1994, a guerrilla leader in the Kandahar region raped and killed three women. A mullah from the frontier area, Mohammed Omar, who was asked by the local people to do something about the outrage, proceeded to recruit a group of religious students, who executed the commander and dispersed his militia. The group then was called upon to deal with other atrocities and started to gain a reputation.

That was the turning point, as Pakistan's leaders started their active support of the Taliban movement with ammunition, fuel, and food. The word *talib* means "religious student"; the Taliban's core and leaders were from Pakistan and Arab countries, while they recruited thousands of refugee students from *madrassas* (religious schools) in Balochistan and the northwest frontier province. The Pakistan-based fanatical religious leaders, with support from Arab nations, identified and targeted the most vulnerable people to build their numbers.

The Taliban also found widespread support among Afghan Pashtuns hostile to local warlords and tired of war and economic instability. By late 1996, the Taliban would capture Kabul, the capital, and gain control of the majority of Afghanistan's thirty-two provinces. Pakistan and Saudi Arabia the first to officially recognize the Taliban government in Kabul. But the Taliban's conservative social practices, justified as being Islamic, did not appeal to Afghanistan's non-Pashtun minorities in the north and west of the country, or to the educated population.

The Taliban's emergence started from the refugee camps of Pakistan and the southern village of Kandahar, but it benefited from many ex–Afghan military officials, as well as expert fighters. The group established extreme discipline in understanding the social and ethnic mixture of the regions it started to penetrate, and it did a very good job of manipulating those ethnic differences for its own political and military gains. The Taliban rewarded those who cooperated and punished those who rejected it. Its major source of financing originated in Pakistan, but the Taliban also capitalized on captured weapons, external military aid, and growing and selling opium to enhance its army.

In the meantime, the Pakistani government and its notorious intelligence agency, ISI, were feverishly engaged in finding ways to influence the chaotic Afghan situation in order to not lose opportunities to open up an overland trade route to central Asia following the Soviets' departure. So Pakistan had a clear hand from the outset in the Taliban emergence in Afghan affairs, despite the country's claims to the contrary. The Taliban's ultimate successes, without a shadow of a doubt, could not have been achieved without direct support from the Pakistani government and ISI. It was also clear that Pakistan acted as a channel for substantial financial assistance from Saudi Arabia and other Arab individuals and governments.

Taliban forces mobilized over thirty thousand fighters within a six-month period. Most of these fighters were allowed to come across from Pakistan; indeed, many were Pakistanis, and their basic training took place in camps not only in southern Afghanistan but also on the Pakistani side of the border. There were, of course, also members of various mujahideen groups who had been heavily recruited, and quite a few paid, Pakistani-trained Taliban soldiers and amateur students.

The Taliban eventually captured Kabul in September 1996 and set itself up as the country's only leadership, amid a clear political gap between the movement and the masses. The decrees the Taliban introduced, which were rooted in the Taliban's political ideology, conflicted with what the group had promised in Kandahar. They introduced religious police, a rigid military campaign against their opponents, and the use of non-Afghan forces.

Since the Soviet invasion of Afghanistan, thousands of non-Afghans had joined the armed struggle against the invaders, eventually making Pakistan and Afghanistan their home while working for al-Qaeda. Aside from thousands of Pakistanis who had attended the religious schools of Pakistan, others came from all over the world, including Egypt, Sudan, Jordan, Palestine, Iraq, Yemen, Algeria, Nigeria,

Morocco, Tanzania, the Philippines, China, Britain, and even the United States. It's safe to say that over one hundred thousand Pakistanis fought in Afghanistan and took their experience back home to tribal areas. These combatants were eventually suspected to be involved in hijackings, kidnappings, and sectarian killings in India, Pakistan, the Middle East, Africa, Europe, and North America.

This use of non-Afghan forces and outlaws from several Middle Eastern Arab countries led by Osama bin Laden started to infuriate and cause doubt among the Afghan people. This caused the Taliban to further rely on foreign support, so the role of bin Laden, who had been an ally of the United States and other countries during the Afghan resistance against invading Russia and other extreme factions from Arab countries, became even more important than before. Simultaneously, the Taliban's grip over 80 percent of the country once again dismantled the social and political bases of many local, regional, and national political parties within Afghanistan. Crushed by the Taliban, the groups became active only outside of Afghanistan and started to operate from neighboring countries.

Meanwhile, the United States considered the Taliban a source of stability that shared anti-Iranian interests with Washington, but the U.S. government misjudged the Taliban's rigid hostility toward modern values in considering Taliban rule the best possible outcome for stability in Afghanistan.

Taliban-imposed policies not only did not fit the Afghan national ideology but actually offended the core traditional values that helped Afghans with different ethnic, religious, and linguistic backgrounds to coexist as a peaceful nation. The group's rigid disrespect for women's rights was seen as particularly offensive to the traditional concept of Afghan honor. The brutality of the Taliban and their non-Afghan, militant friends crippled Afghan civil society, and when a drought hit the country in 2011, people had very few resources, food, or social support on which to draw, which caused even more Afghans to become refugees around the world. The social instability in Afghanistan also diminished the recruitment pool for the Taliban. At the time of this book's printing, about 45 percent of the Taliban forces are non-Afghans.

# He Can't Speak English

FOLLOWING OUR CONTINUED SUPPORT of the Afghan resistance and the news of the Soviets' withdrawal from Afghanistan, it was time to concentrate on our future and on establishing ourselves in America. After moving around quite a bit as a manager to improve the performance of a number of low-performing branches of my bank, I felt it was time for me to step up my game and apply for advanced positions. I made my intentions known to senior management and my regional managers between 1994 and 1995.

I was a little scared to take on this new challenge, but also motivated and extremely energized. I had continually broken production and sales records, earning the respect of my fellow employees and the bank's senior management.

"Are you sure you wish to be a regional manager, Atta?" asked one of my superiors at the time.

"Of course," I said. "I have worked very hard and have done much to learn about banking in general."

My boss looked at me with a little shock and disbelief. I told him I knew exactly what it took to be a regional manager. Promotions to senior positions for people like me were not common at the time—there were not very many minorities at the bank's senior management level—so I knew it was going to be a difficult fight, but I was determined not to give up, and I officially applied for a regional manager position in early 1996.

A senior recruiter at the time told me that I was one of fourteen applicants from across the state of California and that I really needed to prepare well for the interviews.

"That is really good news," I told her.

"Not really," she said. "You don't want too much competition!"

"I love the competition. I am ready for the challenge and can't wait for the interviews to start." The recruiter seemed to really like my attitude and response. I also met with my boss at the time and told him how determined and ready I was.

"Atta, you are not ready yet," were the first words that came out of his mouth.

"What makes you say this?" I asked him with a serious look. I had known my boss for long enough to be convinced that he had some biases against immigrants and foreigners. I had noticed many situations that had made me and several other foreigners uncomfortable at times. While discrimination and workplace harassment policies were established, they were never enforced or adhered to at a time like this one.

I know my boss at the time would be in big trouble in today's workplace environment. He was very abusive in regard to treating certain employees differently, but unfortunately, such behavior was widely exercised during that time.

My boss's relationship with and different treatment of his friends at work was obvious, so I was quite skeptical about a couple of the other manager candidates, from within his circle, with whom I would be competing for the job.

"You are cracking up, Atta—speak louder," my boss ordered during one of his big managers' conference calls, shortly after I had told him about my intention to apply for the regional manager job.

"I am sorry, I will speak louder," I said.

"Can you all hear me okay?" I asked the other managers on the call.

"We can all hear you well, Atta," they replied, so I knew it was only my boss giving me a hard time. I had always been very careful about my voice and tone on conference calls, as I knew I had a deep voice and an accent, but never to the extent that others could not understand me. As a matter of fact, many people, including managers, used to compliment me on my understanding and knowledge of English grammar, so I was quite annoyed and concerned about my boss's first response to my application and his comments on this recent conference call.

Fortunately, by that time I had built a great network of many successful managers, as well as senior management. I was also fortunate to have my name recognized statewide for consistently good performance. So overall I was extremely confident about my performance and successful track record, but I became very concerned about being treated differently in this situation as the thought of discrimination started to sink in.

"Atta can't speak English," one of the applicants for this position said when he had learned of my application. This person was a close friend of my boss and a manager within his region, so I was feeling the pressure and getting very disappointed the more I learned that people were showing direct opposition to my desire to advance within the bank. But I did not even want to approach my boss or this manager about it; I just wanted to get by and make it to an interview with senior recruiters and management. I did plan to be open and up front about my feelings toward my boss and comments made about me at some point, however.

The interview process was tedious and long. Candidates had to go through several steps, including individual and panel interviews with top managers and senior leaders, so word was out about my application for the position among managers throughout the state.

ᘓᒿᘓᒿᘓᒿᘓᒿ

"You made the top-five list," the senior recruiter told me one day, after I had had multiple interviews.

"I am honored and very much looking forward to it," I told her.

"Mr. Broderick himself will be interviewing the final group," she continued. "I am sure you will do quite well; I have heard nothing but great things," she mentioned at the end of our telephone conversation.

This was the moment I had been waiting for, as I simply wanted to make it to this point. My strategy throughout the process had been to be myself and simply share my vision and plans for the responsibility ahead. In the meantime, I had kept my candidacy for this job a secret from my family, in light of my frustration with my boss and his ill feelings toward immigrants; I simply did not want them to be disappointed in case I did not get the job. I thought it was a long shot, anyway, given the ridicule I had endured and the comments made about my qualifications at the time; given this, it would be a great surprise for my family if I did end up getting the position.

ᘓᒿᘓᒿᘓᒿᘓᒿ

I had been informed about an interview three days later, at 10:00 AM, with the president of retail banking in Irvine, California, but I had no plans to fly there that same morning—I was so nervous and excited about this opportunity of a lifetime that I decided to fly to Irvine the night before so as to stay calm and avoid any distraction. I rehearsed and rehearsed lines I had discussed with recruiters, managers, and friends, but ultimately I just decided to follow my natural script and instinct, similar to my approach during my first job application. I knew this interview was the most important one of my career, but still did not see many reasons for changing my strategy. I told myself that the bank and senior management know all about my accomplishments, so I did not have to go over any of them during my interview but rather should focus on my capability to manage people successfully and talk about my good work ethic.

"You have a good story, Atta, but tell me, how you will manage this big position?" was the first thing the bank president asked, after a nice welcome.

"I work harder than anyone I know, and I do not plan to change my work ethic one bit. I have been a leader and managed people since I was eighteen," I told him.

"How did you manage people at such early age?" he asked.

I told him that I had managed my sports team when I was only nineteen years old; I had developed several players, and never had any problem with being a leader.

"I believe people leave their homes to succeed every day, but quite a few managers are not qualified leaders to help them do so," I said. "Workers get blamed a lot, but I think it is the job of a leader to make people succeed," I insisted.

My interview then turned more into a social conversation, as we talked about work ethics in general and how I had been able to implement and execute so many successful plans during my early years of work experience. We also talked a little about incompetent leaders in general around the world and how innocent people fall victim to such weakness. I did not hesitate to talk about the failed leaderships of kings, presidents, and other leaders and their inability to help their decent nations. I simply wanted him to know that I was ready and understood what role I was applying for and that I would not let him and the bank down.

I was back at work the next day as the manager of my bank in San Leandro, California, very happy and convinced that I had accomplished a big task even if I did not get this promotion.

"My God, it is the bank president's office," said a new account person as she ran toward my desk.

"You are a regional manager, Atta" were the first words out of Mr. Broderick's mouth. "We all know you will do a great job. Go celebrate with your family."

My employees at the branch knew I was one of the applicants for the regional manager position in the Central Valley, so my new account employee, Cleo, had remained standing in front of my desk since the bank president's call had come through.

I was stunned and did not know what to say or do next. I buried my head in my two hands as I started to cry, despite customers' and employees' presence. Cleo approached me and put her hand on my shoulder as if something bad had happened. I looked up and told her that I had gotten the job.

"Oh my God!" she yelled, as she hugged me. I then found myself surrounded by my employees and quite a few customers as they heard the news. It was an amazing moment that I will never forget.

I then decided to just go home and inform my mother and family in person.

"I just got a huge promotion as a bank regional manager," I told my wife as I got home. I had told her and my brother in advance to get the family all together but had not yet told my brother what was going on. I wanted to share this moment with all of them together.

"God is great and thank God!" cheered my mother. As she raised her hands in prayer, all of my loved ones and I embraced.

"This one is for you. I have worked very hard for this moment, and now I am a senior manager in America!" I yelled.

It was truly a remarkable night as we enjoyed dinner together, and then it was on to hard work and tackling the new challenge.

"I am simply going to become the best regional manager within this bank," I assured everyone.

With the exception of a few disgruntled competing managers, I started to enjoy amazing support from the bank employees. The news of my appointment spread like wildfire, not so much because I had any special talent as because the first Asian American had been named a bank regional manager. My news was welcomed by everyone, so I became very comfortable and excited about taking on this challenge, and stopped worrying about being ridiculed by a small group—my motivation to do well and prove those few people wrong was stronger than ever.

While covering a large geographical area of Northern California, I had many successful branches within my region, resulting in the bank's receiving prestigious President Club honors in my first year, along with five other branches earning a trip to Maui for being in the bank's top 10 percent of performers. I was feeling really good about my new role, which ultimately led to yet another promotion, to the position of Senior Vice President.

# 9/11

A<small>TTA, WHERE ARE YOU?</small>" one of my managers asked hysterically, as soon as I answered my cell phone while walking toward my car on the morning of September 11, 2001.

"What is going on? I am right in front of my house and leaving for Stockton," I told her.

"Go back and turn on the TV. They hit the Twin Towers," she cried, and said to call her back later.

I hurried back into the house and turned on the TV. There it was—the first plane had hit one of the buildings, and it was burning. I stood there in front of the TV for several moments, stunned as the commentators referred to attacks by the Taliban, Osama bin Laden, and Afghanistan. I thought heard the name Atta somehow, so I turned up the volume to see if I had heard correctly. There, I heard it again: the name of Mohamed Atta, one of the terrorists who had piloted the plane into the World Trade Center.

"Oh, great," I told myself. Of all the names he could have had, the head of this terrorist group had my first name as his last. My strange feelings of guilt, stolen identity, and further worries were overwhelming. It felt like the day I left Afghanistan, sick to my stomach with a sense of loss and pure frustration.

I started yelling and tried to wake up my wife as I stood there in front of the TV. In a matter of moments, I witnessed the second plane crashing into the other tower. My wife and two children rushed downstairs as we all sat there and watched in horror as the attack on the Twin Towers unfolded right in front of our eyes. We never bothered to make our children leave the room, so they, too, watched with us in total shock. We were horrified, and did not know what to say or do as the words "Afghanistan," "bin Laden," and "Taliban" kept on being mentioned.

I wanted to just sit down and watch, but decided to leave for work, as I had a big managers' meeting planned that day at my regional office and felt like staying home was not an option.

I grabbed my briefcase and was heading toward the door when my cell phone rang again. "Are you okay?" asked another manager of mine.

"I am feeling completely sick," I told her, "but I am heading to the office and will see you there."

"Don't leave the house," I instructed my wife.

"Dad, please be careful!" yelled my son. "Why don't you stay home?" he asked.

I gave him another hug and told him I had a meeting planned and had to go to work.

I drove off, trying to turn on various radio stations in hopes of gathering new information, but there it was again, nothing but talk about attacks guided from inside Afghanistan, with various comments surrounding my homeland, the Taliban, and al-Qaeda.

I decided to call my mother, who started crying as soon as she heard my voice. She asked why I was driving and told me I should be staying home. I told her I had a big meeting and was responsible for managing hundreds of people, so I did not have a choice.

"Be careful, then," she said.

"We have nothing to be afraid of, Mother," I told her.

"I heard they were all Arabs," she mentioned.

"Yes, thank God there is no mention of any Afghan terrorists so far," I assured her.

"Did you hear the name?" she asked.

I knew she was referring to the name Mohamed Atta. I told her I had heard.

"Well, some people just don't care—we are all in danger now," she said.

I tried to assure her we were going to be okay, but I could hear her sobbing as she asked me to try and get hold of my sister in New York. I started calling my sister and brother-in-law, who both worked in downtown New York, but I kept getting a busy signal. By the time I finished my half-hour drive to work, I had called most of my immediate family members and had advised them all to be extremely careful about their surroundings.

After entering the underground parking garage of my bank's building, I noticed increased security presence right away as I quickly parked the car and anxiously ran up the stairs. I rushed to the front of a line standing before a security desk to talk to the security guard, Ali, who was a native of Pakistan and a very smart and pleasant man; we loved to talk about politics and events in our home countries whenever we had opportunities.

Right away, he came out from behind his counter area and gave me a big hug in front of everyone. It was sort of a weird feeling, as I did not want to make it look like it was a celebratory hug but rather a shared sense of loss and despair.

My administrative assistant also gave me a hug as I cried in her arms for a few minutes while telling her how bad I felt.

"You have nothing to be ashamed of, Atta," she said.

"I know, but it really hurts." I told her not only how devastating this attack was for us as Americans but what it really meant for Afghans.

To my surprise, as all the managers started to arrive, each one gave me a hug and cried. I had developed great relationships with my regional employees and everyone throughout our organization and felt supported. However, I was worried about my family and Afghans in general. How would people's perceptions of us change? We had enjoyed enormous support and been received with open arms within American society so far, but what now?

"We need to keep going and not cave in," stated one of my managers, Joe, as he gave me a big hug while stating his position firmly again: "We need to take our fight there. We are Americans." It was a brave but unsettling statement.

"What do you think, Atta?" one of the managers asked.

"I am so sorry." I broke into tears then, unable to say another word. The room became completely silent as I just stood there in front of my team.

"I know how you feel," said Joe, as he put his hand on my shoulder.

I wasn't sure why, but I felt a sense of responsibility and regret, so it felt good to apologize, but at the same time I felt terrible even hearing my home country's name associated with this tragedy.

"I am so happy you have shared so many of your Afghan stories, but we would love to hear your perspective. How could they have launched such an attack from so far away?" commented one manager.

"I will be happy to explain later, but for now just want to say that Afghans have long felt the danger of losing control of our country to Arab outlaws, so this is not the work of Afghans," I told everyone. "I believe you should all go back to your branches rather than be here," I continued.

"No, we've got to be brave and not be afraid," Joe said.

"It is not about being afraid or caving to terrorists, but your teams would rather see you in your branches," I told them.

In the early afternoon, my admin rushed to my office to inform me that the retail bank's senior manager was on the phone. She normally transferred calls, but she was too excited about this one because she had never spoken to the senior manager before, so she wanted to inform me personally.

"Are you okay, Atta?" he asked right after I said hello.

"I am fine, sir," I said, but then I could not contain myself and burst into tears. "I am so sorry—I am okay, but I am filled with an incredible sense of loss and guilt," I continued.

"But you have nothing to do with this, Atta. Why are you feeling guilty?" he asked.

"I'm not sure, but I know the attacks were initiated from my homeland, Afghanistan. I feel awful," I told him.

"You are a very proud Afghan American, Atta, and we are all very proud of you. I just called to make sure you are okay," he continued

"This means a lot, sir. I truly appreciate it," I told him.

"Please go home to your family and give them my regards and hugs," he continued.

After we hung up, I sobbed for the next few minutes. To have received a call from someone of Mike's stature meant the world to me. I realized my great friends at the bank were all feeling badly, knowing I had come from Afghanistan and hearing the name Atta in association with the terrorist group responsible for the World Trade Center attacks.

By later that afternoon, the media had completely taken over and everyone's radio had resorted to news, but it was still all too much to grasp. As I drove on Highway 5, I realized things were moving as usual; hundreds of cars were heading north as people returned home from their daily routines, and for a moment it seemed as if life was going on as usual. It was a little comforting in the midst of my feeling like the lives of Afghans would never again be the same here or anywhere around the world, because our decent reputation had been tarnished in the worst imaginable way.

As I made it to my neighborhood in Tracy, where quite a few Afghan families lived, I hoped to see someone just to talk to before going home. I had not spoken to any Afghans except for members of my family and a few close friends so far, so I intentionally made a big loop around the lake in hopes of finding someone else I could talk to in person, but there were no Afghans in the area. I quickly realized this was actually not a good time to be outside; it was time to stay home and not show your face to anyone.

"Are you sure we are going to be okay, Dad?" my son asked as soon as I entered the house and gave my family a big hug. I had been worried about him all day; I was not sure how he would be treated and what was going on in his school, where he was a sixth-grader. I had told my wife to be prepared to pick him up in case he was uncomfortable.

"So, what happened there? How was your day, son?" I asked.

"Wow, it was a bad day, very sad, Dad—all I heard about was Arab terrorists. I am really confused," he stated. "But why are you guys worried? This has nothing to do with us," he said.

He told us the people at school had been very nice as they talked about the attacks on the World Trade Center and actually played news clips, while also telling students that counselors were available to talk about the events. He felt pretty good about the level of support from school and his fellow students but was still visibly shaken because of his status as an Afghan American.

"What does this have to with Afghanistan? Why Afghanistan?" he questioned nervously.

"Yes, these terrorists were all Arabs and no Afghan terrorists were involved, but it is quite complicated story, son; I need to explain things a little," I said.

Then I whispered in his ear, "We need to be careful, son, as we don't want to scare your little sister."

I then sat with him for half an hour and explained what had happened to Afghanistan during the last decade, as well as discussing the impact of Osama bin Laden, al-Queda, and the Taliban. I felt it was important for him to understand the connection. He was as confused as any American would have been, except for the people who had followed Afghanistan and the Taliban during the few years prior to these attacks. I knew there was too much information there for my son to understand but felt it was extremely important for him to know it anyway, as he had to face reality and probably explain his position and identity to his friends and classmates. I told him not to be afraid to talk about what he knew and to help distinguish his position from that of terrorists and extremists.

During the evening of 9/11, I turned on the radio to hear about Bay Area reactions to the attacks, knowing there would be lots of chatter in light of the big Afghan community in the area. One of the first comments by a prominent radio station was "Bomb Afghanistan, bomb them all, why should we care about the loss of people who didn't care about us?" As if the innocent people of Afghanistan had bombed the World Trade Center?

I was devastated and wanted to call the station, but realized the host might be just another naive individual who had no clue about the real cause and criminals behind these attacks. I simply wanted to let him know that it was really not the fault of decent Afghan people but the direct result of poor leadership and bad decisions by superpowers.

Yes, my beloved homeland suddenly found itself in the eye of a global storm. Despite worldwide discussions and news about Osama bin Laden and his network being responsible for the 9/11 attacks, there was a clear message about and connection to the word "Afghanistan" because of the fact that the culprits were based there and protected by the Taliban government. Afghanistan quickly became the focus of an American-led campaign to go after bin Laden and his network of destruction, using mainly air power. As a result, the innocent people of Afghanistan were undergoing still more suffering, privation, and displacement, similar to what they had endured over the course of the past two decades.

After the morning of September 11, I could not stop telling anyone and everyone that Arabs and other non-Afghans associated with al-Qaeda under Osama bin Laden who had been based in Afghanistan were the ones responsible for the catastrophic terrorist attacks. It just felt good to do so. It had become a natural reaction for me and every Afghan I knew, as we realized not many people had any idea about Afghanistan and al-Qaeda and could not make the connections. While I was truly sad about the loss of so many lives and the destruction of the Twin Towers, I saw it as my responsibility to talk about the real causes and people behind the attacks—to explain that they had roots in militant warfare that originated in the Middle

East, and tell people about how the U.S. and the Western world's involvement in political, economic, and military engagement had been important in the development of a rigid political environment shaping this new brand of global militancy.

After a couple of very anxious weeks at work, as things were returning to some level of normalcy, I was informed I had to attend a senior-level management meeting in Seattle. I was getting increasingly uncomfortable day by day after hearing the name Atta repeatedly in the media, so the idea of going through airport security on this trip was quite daunting. I decided to schedule a meeting with my boss to let him know about my fears of traveling to Seattle, or anywhere, at that point.

"I am so sorry, Atta, but you have nothing to worry about," he mentioned right off the bat. "Book your flight with your other fellow managers. I can see your concern about traveling alone at this point, but I don't think you will have any difficulty and I do want you to go. I believe everyone will be quite happy to see you there in Seattle, so let's book the flight, Atta," he continued, as he patted me on the shoulder.

I left my home in Tracy hours before the flight for the long drive to the Sacramento airport. I just wanted to keep on driving, as the thought of having the same name as the 9/11 mastermind Mohamed Atta and dealing with all the security and suspicion about Middle Eastern and Asian people was really overwhelming me. A few times I caught myself driving very slowly and oftentimes bothering drivers behind me. I just did not want to be anywhere in public these days, but rather at work or with my family.

Once inside the terminal, I was once again struck with an amazing feeling of paranoia that people would look at me with suspicion and curiosity. As I started walking toward the long security line, I was hoping to see a colleague from the bank whom I could talk to. Typically there would be at least a few colleagues traveling from Sacramento to Seattle, but I could not see anyone within these lines.

After a long delay, I made it to the security checkpoint and handed over both my ticket confirmation, which had my nickname, Atta, and my last name on it, and my driver's license, which showed my full first name, Attaullah, followed by my middle name and then my last name, so the agent looked puzzled and I started to worry. He asked why the two documents did not match.

I told him that I had used only the shortened version of my first name for a long time in the United States in order to make it easier at work and in other interactions with Americans. He politely accepted my explanation, but I still thought that I would be one of the targeted passengers for screening, until he pointed me to go through the regular metal detector. Within minutes, I was out of the area and felt as if I had just been released from jail.

With a big sigh of relief, I felt happy and energized again. I moved on toward the gate area but realized there were still many curious eyes staring, which I had accepted as being simply a fact of life at the time. Despite the awkwardness, I decided not to take it personally and to instead respect people's curiosity.

I was fortunately accompanied by at least four colleagues from the bank, which made me very comfortable. They were all so gracious and kind, giving me big hugs while asking about me and my family. They all knew that I had come from Afghanistan years back, and they showed their genuine respect and support for me, especially in front of these hundreds of other passengers. I felt much better as we started to interact and talk about business a little, but almost all conversations quickly turned to Afghanistan. I had no problem talking about my experience and all my frustration about Afghanistan since the Russian departure, and about how innocent people were still victims in the hands of outsiders, ultimately even the Arab terrorists who contributed to the 9/11 attacks.

Our lives since 9/11 have never been the same. While the small American group invasion drove the Taliban out of Kabul and the city's immediate surroundings, the people of Afghanistan have continued to suffer from feelings of undeserved guilt about having housed the Taliban and some of the 9/11 attackers in their homeland.

Afghans have continued to observe 9/11 and the loss of innocent lives. As I sat at home alongside my family members in September 2011 and listened to the names of victims being cited by their children and family members, I wondered when there will be a day when the names of the millions of decent Afghans who have lost their lives during the last thirty-plus years are read.

# Returning Home

$After$ I decided to write this memoir, I wanted to travel to my homeland in search of the truth about what has happened there. I had watched, heard, and learned about the destruction of millions of people, many of whom did not even receive the proper burial they deserved. The patriotic blood of decent Afghan people had been spilled all over the country for no good reason.

At the request of my longtime friend Ahmad, we decided to travel together to Afghanistan on January 11, 2011.

"I think we are at the wrong gate," I told Ahmad during an eight-hour layover in Dubai, which we had flown to from San Francisco.

"No, this is it," he said, laughing and giving me a sarcastic look.

"Look at the people! I don't see a single Afghan here," I said, as I looked around the crowded gate area full of what I considered foreigners.

"That is right; most foreigners take this early flight," he said. "But look at the corner; there are at least five Afghans I can see."

I was starting to feel really sad. Not that I would not have welcomed foreigners to our homeland, but this was not what I expected, and the thought of seeing our country run again by foreigners blurred my vision at the moment.

"But what about all the Afghan experts around the world who could help?" I asked.

"You need to cool off and stop asking so many questions. You will learn more when we get there—relax," he told me with a smirk on his face.

But I could not stop worrying and looking around; I wanted to see who these people were and where they were coming from. There were quite a few Americans, including military and private security personnel, Europeans, men and women of Asian and Indian descent, and even a few German police in uniform, which looked really odd; I wondered why German police would be traveling in uniform. I simply could not stop looking around, and felt exactly the way I had felt thirty years ago at the Frankfurt airport—lost and looking at everyone as if they were from another planet.

I had suddenly become a curious observer, and was trying to register everything I was seeing for my book notes. I was planning to videotape my entire trip starting the moment I boarded the plane, but I suspected that I could not possibly turn my camcorder on with all these foreigners and security personnel around. I asked Ahmad, since he had traveled to and from Afghanistan a few times recently.

"Only if you want to be dead now," he said with a broad smile.

"Okay, I guess I can start taping when we get there, then," I told him.

"But not outside the plane or inside the airport," he warned me. He told me I might be able to start once we were out of the Kabul airport, but said never to film military and security personnel. I was not happy about his response at all, but I realized I had no choice.

We were finally on our way to visit my homeland again after thirty years. I was so happy that we were taking the 6:30 AM flight, as I simply wanted to look around and see everything for as long as I could. I stared down at the countryside from my window seat. As the pilot announced our descent into Kabul, I noticed how dense the city looked from above. I remembered it as a city occupied by only 150,000–200,000 people when I left in the early 1980s. By many estimates, Kabul was now home to over five million people. It looked busy and spectacular because of snowfall from just the night before. From the air it looked like the old Kabul, with vibrant and beautiful mountains and snow-covered hilltops.

The airport seemed nothing like the old one. The area had been beaten up quite badly during the years of war, and whereas the airport used to house merely two or three planes at one time, now I noticed a dozen transport planes.

"I am sorry, but I have to take some video," I told Ahmad, as I reached into my bag to pull out my camcorder.

"I don't think that's a good idea," he shouted, but I just went and turned the camera on before taking the stairs down from the plane. I then saw security personnel with walkie-talkies standing on both sides of the stairs and carefully examining passengers. I simply kept filming, though I did not take aim directly at them, and kept on walking. I knew I was being watched carefully, but to my surprise, no one said anything until we reached the doorstep of customs.

We were then inside the so-called new Kabul International Airport. So much had been made of this project, sponsored by the Japanese government, that I had expected a modern airport similar to at least some other, decent international airports. This new structure pretty much resembled the old one, and looked to me like a project that was only half-completed. The entry to customs was very small by today's standards, with only eight booths that looked like outdoor ticket booths. The ceiling was uncovered, with visible wires.

We lined up with hundreds of other foreigners and very few Afghans in front of only three open booths, each one guarded by a uniformed police officer. As I got closer to the booth, the officer standing in front of me started talking and asked if I was there for the first time. I was not sure why he would figure that I was a first-timer there, but the fact that I was Afghan seemed to make him happy. He immediately pointed to the passenger at the booth in front of me and started cursing him in a whisper. I started to feel very uncomfortable. The guard went on to tell me that this guy was in and out of Kabul every week and that he was one of the traitors who were selling information about Afghanistan and its people.

"You see all these Americans and foreigners?" he asked.

"Of course, there are thousands of them here," I said.

"We need them here. Our own government is very corrupt, and no one in it can be trusted. They are all crooks. Things are so bad, we would die within months without these people," he said.

"I hope they leave, but not so soon that I don't see any return to the old days and our Afghan pride," he continued, his eyes beginning to water. "Who will remain in charge if the Americans and other foreign troops leave?"

The passenger in front of me at the booth moved away, and it was my turn.

"Why are you here?" the customs officer asked rudely, making no gesture of courtesy, not even a "hello" or *"salaam."*

"I am here to visit family and friends," I told him.

"Come from America?" he asked.

"Yes," I said.

"How about Dubai?" he asked.

I told him that I had originally traveled from America, with a short stay in Dubai. He then gave me a very dirty look as he punched numbers silently into his computer for several minutes.

"Go" was the only word that then came out of his mouth.

I was devastated by this treatment, as I had never expected such behavior from an Afghan before. I remembered only great manners and hospitality during my upbringing toward people. I wondered what had happened to those times when every guest used to be treated as a king.

After gathering our belongings, Ahmad and I started to walk toward the exit doors. My heart pounded as we left the building. There we were. I stood still for a few minutes while the two porters and Ahmad walked away toward the sideline. I just wanted to breathe Kabul's air. It felt very cold and crisp, and reminded me of the good old snowy days in the city. The porters told me we were very lucky, as the snowfall the night before had really cleaned up the dirty Kabul air.

"What are you doing?" yelled Ahmad, when he saw me standing there. I joined him and the two porters and started walking in front of the old terminal, seeing a security checkpoint every one hundred feet. The area seemed like a militarized zone, with armored cars moving in and out of the area as they maneuvered through cement barricades. I was so caught up in the moment that I almost forgot to pull out my video camera. When I did, Ahmad warned me once again to exercise caution. I was happy I had brought a very small, new camcorder that could easily fit in the palm of my hand. I started using it sneakily, not holding it up as I would a regular camera, so as to avoid any objection from military and security personnel. At the times when I did dare to hold the camera up right in front of me, I could see several army personnel and security guards who did not seem to be amused.

As we left the parking lot, our cab driver started playing an old song and asked if we were visiting for the first time. I told him I was returning after thirty years, so he was very happy to welcome me back and starting talking. I informed him that I wished to videotape my experience in Kabul and asked if he had any objection.

"Not at all," he answered, as he drove us along the very crowded highway.

"This is no longer the Afghanistan you knew, my friend," he said, as I turned the camera from side to side in order to capture the images of people, shops, and the crowded city. Nothing looked the same! The car barely moved as it tried to maneuver through an incredibly busy street full of cars, carts, and people. This stretch of highway used be surrounded by occasional small neighborhoods, but now the entire stretch from the airport to the center of the city was filled with homes, stores, and crowded open markets.

"This is now a country of thieves," he said.

"Wow, sorry to hear it, my friend," I said to encourage him a little, with my camera still running, as I simply wanted to hear the facts from regular people like this cab driver.

"Yes, they have been ripping us apart for more than thirty years, and there is no end," he went on.

"Well, but I thought things were better these days," I mentioned.

"You have got to be kidding," he said. "Things are very good for the thieves and commanders, of course, but not for ordinary people. I have seen it all, my friend, and I am more scared now than ever. It used to be all about war and killing, but it is now about our country losing its identity, and so I am scared for my children. I have nine children and plan to take them out of Afghanistan, not for the purpose of safety but because I don't want them to grow up under these conditions, with no sense of pride and dignity. This is a corrupt society with fake leaders and dangerous warlords who care only for themselves and have no interest in our well-being," he sighed.

"Let me show you just a few examples; I know your friends will show you a lot, but let me take you through this street," he continued, as he turned right onto a bumpy dirt road leading toward some big homes not too far from the area.

"Look at these monster buildings," he shouted, as I continued filming both sides of the road. It was absolutely insane! A group of army or security personnel stood in front of almost every house, and every gate and entry was barricaded with heavy cement blocks.

"Security jobs are here," I mentioned to the driver.

"Oh, yes! This is the number-one job inside Afghanistan; it seems like half of the people are either in military or security uniforms," he replied, laughing.

"Keep the camera away from the window, as these are all homes of warlords, most of which have been turned into office buildings," he continued.

He kept on driving for a couple miles and got back on the main highway. The cab driver sounded extremely upset, but he showed no fear about speaking his mind.

This whole drive from the airport to the center of Kabul was one big adventure, filled with a mixture of curiosity and frustration.

☙❧☙❧☙❧

A ten-minute drive from the airport to our hotel, known as the Kabul Serena Hotel, had become so much more difficult than in the past. Due to the hotel's proximity to the defense ministry, old palace, and

U.S. bases in the area, the roadways around it had become almost completely blocked.

"We are here," Ahmad said happily as the car finally pulled up on the side of a very busy road near the hotel gate. I first thought it was another military compound because of the presence of dozens of armed personnel, but looking at the building carefully, I realized it was the old Kabul Hotel, still standing, with its original concrete walls and solid structure.

"Why can't we drive inside the hotel yard?" I asked.

"They only allow authorized cars inside; you have to go through a heavy security checkpoint first," Ahmad answered.

Once we were past the armed security guards, we were led inside the yard through a small door and into a security checkpoint, next to a big iron door blocked by a very heavy iron gate operated by more security guards, who allowed cars in and out of the hotel. We were then guided into a room equipped with a metal detector. The room was packed with six or seven guards, including two women, who were responsible for female body searches. Our luggage was carefully checked through a big detector, and we were then subjected to a full-body search.

Finally, there it was! The old Kabul Hotel, now the Kabul Serena Hotel, had been turned into a true five-star establishment with great decorations, an immaculate lobby, and professionally dressed employees. The entire hotel was closely guarded inside and outside, with armed civilian guards in almost every corner, along with video cameras, so that made me feel good about security.

"Spectacular," I sighed as we started to tour the hotel. One of the first areas I wanted to see was the hall where we had attended many weddings and engagements during our high school days. The hall had now been redecorated and equipped with exquisite furniture and decorations. I was told the hall was now mainly used by Afghan's elite and for official meetings. I was also warned not to turn on my camera anywhere in the rooms or halls, but I honestly could not resist and did not think I would hurt anyone if I took a few shots here and there, only for the purpose of sharing them with family and friends in America.

"Do you know how much we are going to pay here per night?" I asked Ahmad. He had been joking around about the price ever since I had asked him to find a place to stay in Kabul. I had informed him that I had a ton of relatives and would be very comfortable staying with my uncles and cousins, but he had insisted on a central location from which we could visit with everyone while avoiding traffic hassles. Now I was concerned, because I had heard about the outrageous rates at Kabul hotels, well above the average cost of a hotel even in the United States or Europe.

"Well, you are at a great place, so don't complain," Ahmad said.

"I'm not complaining—just give me an idea, at least, now that we have a double bedroom," I said.

"I am a member here and get great discounts, so we are good." Ahmad still would not tell me, so I finally gave up and realized he was acting as a host and did not feel it was important for me to pay anything, even though I had every intention of paying my share. I then found out the average cost for a single room ran US$300–400 per night. That just blew me away, as I could not see any justification for such exorbitant expense within such a poor country as Afghanistan, but this was yet another indication of the difference that exists between ordinary ranks of people and the wealthy elite.

Around noon, we went to the main restaurant for lunch. It was filled with almost ninety foreigners, as well as some Afghan men and women wearing professional attire. I again had very mixed feelings and continued to question the presence of so many foreigners and very few Afghans within the business community. This particular hotel was definitely a gathering place for businesses, as well as many NGOs, and ultimately a place to discuss government and corporate deals. "You have to be careful, Atta, as there are a ton of government personnel within this hotel," Ahmad mentioned, as we were led to the only two open seats.

After a great buffet, full of every possible Afghan food and a selection of American and European dishes, we headed out to the lobby, where things looked very different than they had at the time of our arrival that morning.

"What is going on?" I asked, as we looked around to see the entire lobby full of people dressed mostly in suits, along with quite a few armed guards and even a few American soldiers.

"Sit here and let me find out," Ahmad said, as he proceeded toward the reception area.

"It's a birthday party for the daughter of a government official," he explained when he came back, a smirk on his face.

"You have got to be kidding me," I said, feeling both amused and disturbed by the news.

"No, I am not kidding," Ahmad replied. "Actually, there are at least four to five other ministers and many government and businesspeople attending the birthday luncheon right there inside the wedding hall."

"Well, then, I am staying here to watch," I told him.

"I like that idea; plus, a good business friend of mine is also at this party, so maybe we'll be able to talk to him when they come out," Ahmad agreed.

"Okay, let's just kill some time. Can I go get my camera?" I asked.

"No way," he said.

"Wow, what do you think they are paying for such a party?" I asked.

"Well, money is not an issue for these people; there is plenty of cash in everyone's pocket," Ahmad answered.

"But look—it is not just about the number of people attending the party; the lobby is full of bodyguards and armed personnel," I said. "This place now looks like a military hall." I was getting more agitated by the minute.

"Look outside, at the courtyard area and parking lot," Ahmad said.

The whole area was filled with soldiers and guards, standing and chatting around their vehicles.

"Just walk around as if you are waiting for someone and stop looking curious," Ahmad warned me. I then started to walk toward the hotel entrance, pretending I was waiting for someone, so that I could get a better look at the courtyard. There were at least a dozen luxury SUVs parked alongside military-style jeeps, guarded by dozens of soldiers and security personnel. It was an amazing and bizarre sight to be inside a five-star hotel with hundreds of foreign and Afghan business personnel and see this military presence outside. I was very sad to witness firsthand the lavish lifestyle of a few at the expense of millions of decent Afghans who struggled to eat one meal per day.

# Praying with the Taliban

P<small>RIOR TO ARRIVING IN</small> K<small>ABUL</small>, I had informed my first cousin about my intention to go to my parents' and grandparents' village, Arghandi, and visit my father's grave. My parents had actually adopted this cousin, Rashidudin, when he had lost his father at an early age, so I could not think of a better person to accompany me on this big first journey outside of Kabul.

After a night filled with anticipation, I got a call from my cousin in the early morning informing me that he and his son would be arriving soon. He also said that if I had brought any traditional Afghan clothing, I should wear it.

"Do you have a hat?" he asked.

"No, why do I need to put on a hat?" I asked him.

"Well, we are going to be outside of Kabul and in the villages, so it's very important for you to wear something. I brought an additional one with me just in case," he assured me.

It was a perfect Kabul winter Friday—with very bright sun, but extremely cold in early morning—but I had prepared well by bringing a pair of thermal leggings and a big, warm jacket. I intentionally had a jacket with big pockets that could hide my camera, so that I could avoid looking like a journalist.

As I left the hotel compound and stood by the side of the road, a car pulled up and I quickly recognized my cousin and his son. They stopped the car and immediately got out to give me a hug, but it felt weird, as the hotel guards kept on walking toward the car as if we were wasting too much time getting in. The guards knew I was a guest, but they did not seem to care for seeing us parked there for a long time.

Once I was inside the car and saw my cousin Rashidudin, we both started crying. It had been an incredibly tough year for our entire family, as a result of Zia's death. The fact that Zia had married Rashidudin's daughter only made it harder to see my cousin now.

Shortly after the Russians' defeat and withdrawal in 1989, after over ten years of heroic fighting for the freedom of Afghanistan, my brother Zia had joined our family in the United States. He later returned to Afghanistan to marry and ultimately brought his wife to America, too.

While happily working as an Oakland cab driver and enjoying life with his wife and three beautiful kids, Zia was abruptly and without any serious warning signs diagnosed with a cancerous tumor in July 2009. He ultimately lost his fight against cancer in February 2010; his wife and children continue to live with my mother in Alameda.

We drove through half of Kabul on our way to the village of Arghandi, about eighteen kilometers away. Rashidudin had informed me that my father's only remaining cousin, Abdul Rahim, had asked to join us, so we headed to Karte Sakhi district to pick him up. It was a perfect opportunity to travel through the city without much delay, as Friday is the official holiday of the week. Within half an hour we were at the foot of an area where we used to go watch skiing in the early 1970s. Although it was limited to a privileged few, there had been a great ski lodge with spectacular views, overlooking the main highway connecting Kabul to the east of Afghanistan and the beautiful Arghandi valley.

"Get ready for the bumpy ride!" yelled Rashidudin, while pointing to the unpaved road we used to take to the village.

"Wow, it still looks the same!" I commented. The road looked as if not a single piece of dirt had moved since I had last been on it.

"Except for the bridge ahead," Rashidudin mentioned.

"Who built the new bridge?" I asked.

"Oh, it was during Taliban rule; somehow they approved the construction of a bridge that has held up ever since," he explained.

"Well, they did something for Arghandi," Abdul Rahim said.

Meanwhile, I continued to record the scene with my video camera. I was very motivated to take a snapshot of everything—every moment and movement—despite the bumpy ride. I did not care what I filmed; as we moved I pointed the camera at both sides of the road and into the wilderness until, eventually, human beings and animals appeared. The farmland along the road looked deserted and dry, covered with a layer of white snow. It looks as if no one ever grew anything there anymore.

"Do people still farm on these lands?" I asked Rashidudin.

"Oh, yes. It has been quite dry for a long time, but they try their best," he replied.

"But what happened to all the trees around? I asked.

"What do you expect?" he said. "People have been using every piece of wood they can get their hands on for heating."

We kept on driving along the same one-lane dirt road that we used to walk on—or, at times, ride donkeys on—years ago. As we got closer and closer to the village, I was feeling really anxious, anticipating big changes, but it wasn't to be. With the exception of a few newer buildings here and there, the village looked very much the same as it had thirty years earlier, with hundreds of mud homes surrounded by big walls. Children played outside their homes, and a few young men congregated, playing traditional street games. The main difference I saw was the number of cars parked at the entrance of the village: at least twenty cargo and passenger cars, all parked around the big lot. We used to see only one or two cars coming and going each day, but nowadays there were dozens.

"There it is." My cousin pointed to our garden/yard as the car pulled up to a green door.

"What happened to the big old door?" I questioned.

"Well, it collapsed one winter, so we replaced it with this new one," he said.

"But why such ugly colors?" I asked angrily, realizing the door did not match the big mud wall and the makeup of the village at all. I had seen the same changes all around the city of Kabul, too.

"These are not our Afghan colors," I commented. I had by then noticed homes in Kabul and on the way with mainly dark green, yellow, and brown colors, similar to homes in Pakistan.

"Wow, they even changed our true colors," I told them with much frustration. My relatives knew I was not happy at all. As we entered the garden that had been home for hundreds of years to Arghandiwal generations, I started taking pictures and shooting videos. But it looked so bare; none of the tall walnut, apple, and cherry trees existed anymore. I was devastated, but kept on turning the camera around in hopes of finding a decent tree or object that I could take photos of.

"My goodness, did you guys even have to cut the trees inside the garden?" I asked angrily.

"No, no, we were not living here during those difficult days," my cousin said. "Our family farmers lived here during communist and Taliban rule." He went on to say that these farmers had had no other means of heating their homes during the war, so they had eventually had to cut the trees to survive. The former garden had been green—full of various fruit trees and beautiful flowers, with no visible dirt around—but now it was nothing but dirt.

"I am so sorry, Atta," Rashidudin said. He came closer and put his hand on my shoulder as he pointed to a couple of new rooms built in the corner of the big garden, informing me that Zia had built this unit during the war years to house his fighters. I moved closer as we all started crying, wanting to get a mental picture of my brother taking care of his fighters at night.

"I am not letting anyone live in it," Rashidudin's son added, while wiping away his tears. "We will keep it unoccupied for as long as it takes."

"Yes, I agree! We should keep it open and clean but unoccupied," I told him. The little house, with its bathroom and all the other amenities of a village structure, seemed like a sacred place now, so we agreed to preserve it in memory of Zia and his ten-year fight against the Russians.

It was then time to go inside our home, where generations of Arghandiwals had lived. We entered through the same door that I remembered from thirty years ago, as I set the camera rolling again. There it was! Aside from a few minor changes and patches here and there, the village home looked intact.

"Well, seems like Arghandi is the only place that has not been bombed," I noted.

"Oh, no, these homes are the survivors," Abdul Rahim said, explaining that the village, particularly in the higher hills and mountain areas, had been bombed numerous times during and after the Russian invasion.

"They sent helicopters to search for guerilla fighters all over," Rashidudin added.

We then had lunch along with at least ten of the village elders, inside the same room we used to sleep in years earlier. The village food tasted as good as ever as we all sat around a big plastic table and talked about their horrifying experiences. Despite all the war and devastation they had seen, they still sounded positive and optimistic. I felt quite weak compared with these men, who had lost many members of their families and children over the years but somehow continued to be determined. They even continued to praise the Taliban! Everyone had nothing but good things to say about them, as they were particularly grateful for the safety and security the Taliban had provided for them during their rule.

"No one would dare steal a penny," one mentioned. "They were very strict, but their rule was a rule."

After our hearty meal and tea, it was time to prepare for the big Friday prayer at the center of village. "No filming or showing the camera there," said Abdul Rahim.

"I wish I could, but I realize it is very dangerous to do so," I assured him. I stashed the camera in my big jacket.

"There will be a ton of Taliban fighters present, but you will be okay," Rashidudin said. I was honestly not afraid at all, but rather anxious to see these soldiers up close and even have a chance to talk with them.

We started walking toward a big mosque that had been built during the last few years and found ourselves surrounded by hundreds of villagers exchanging greetings. "What a sight!" I thought; old and young people were all dressed in traditional Afghan clothes. The majority wore turbans, but a few wore round hats made of wool or karakul sheepskin. The crowd was making its way toward the mosque, but many people respectfully stopped to greet our group of visitors.

We took our shoes off and entered the big mosque. It was well-heated and smelled very good, as if someone had sprayed the room with nice perfume. With the mosque almost full, we sat in our prayer lanes as the imam delivered a speech about character and care of the needy. He then announced the donation process and explained how important it was for people to give in order to help others within the community.

We prayed together with hundreds of people stacked shoulder to shoulder inside, while at least a hundred more lined up to pray outside the mosque under a beautiful and sunny but cold afternoon sky. It was a great sight to see people of all ages from the village come together and pray. Speakers broadcasting the imam's sermon ensured that most villagers could hear it easily.

My cousin had made arrangements for us to meet with the imam, who had been very close to my late brother, and with a few Taliban fighters, so we stayed inside until most people had vacated the mosque. We then walked over and exchanged greetings with the imam, who was an imposing figure—about six-foot-two, with a long beard and wearing a neat, high-quality traditional dress. He looked to be in his late forties, but had the respect of everyone there.

The imam led us into an adjoining room, where at least twenty other people joined us. According to Afghan tradition, he and others insisted that we take a place at the head of the room, which was furnished with carpeted mattresses and pillows.

"The young men with dark turbans in the room are members of the local Taliban," whispered my cousin. I started to look around and realized there were indeed at least fifteen people with dark turbans and long beards. They kept looking at me as though I had come from a different planet. The imam then gathered everyone's attention as he started reciting verses of the Quran in honor of Zia, followed by the recitation of another verse by a young member sitting at the far end of the room. Right after a long prayer, the imam started to tell people about my brother and what a great resistance fighter he had been. He described Zia's sacrifices over the years and thanked my family for supporting the freedom fighters during the war. I was feeling very emotional. I had become more susceptible to crying since Zia's death, and would simply break into tears whenever I heard his name, but this was no place for me to shed them, as I could not afford to appear weak in the presence of this tough crowd.

It was then my turn to thank everyone and share our family pride and honor in having a brother like Zia.

"Yes, I did not have the honor to fight alongside him, but we heard he was a true, legitimate mujaheed," mentioned one young man. This was followed by comments from a few other men around the room, as the young Taliban listened but continued to look at me with curiosity.

It took a good half hour to say goodbye to everyone, including the imam, as we exchanged hugs and best wishes and then left for a mile-long walk alongside the mountain to visit my father's and ancestors' graves. I was accompanied by at least a dozen relatives and friends as we walked. The scene was simply spectacular, with mountains half covered with fresh snow under a clear blue sky. It was Afghan nature at its best. I wanted to just walk and enjoy the weather, but within minutes I was down on my knees with my hands on my father's grave, which had been marked and protected by solid rock and cement. I cried and cried for many minutes before my cousin and relatives tried to drag me away, but I insisted on staying longer. This was one of the most satisfying moments of my life; I felt grateful to have made it there and paid my respects once again.

"So, tell me about all these young Taliban," I said to Rashidudin as we started to walk away from the cemetery. "How come there are so many of them around, and so close to the capital?"

My cousin and other relatives started to tell me that there were actually tons of Taliban and other religious groups in the area who were not happy with the current corrupt government of Afghanistan. These young fighters were very easy prey for recruitment by the Taliban and other groups for very little money in order to make a living.

*View of the village of Arghandi from my father's gravesite, December 2010.*

"These young men have no education and no hope for jobs, and they are getting paid very well by the Taliban, so what would stop them from joining these groups? They believe their country is being invaded by Americans now, similar to how they felt about Russians! They don't see any difference," he said.

He then told me that the young Taliban recruits, even those within close proximity of the capital, got very good support from their leaders, including money, clothing, and constant lectures and training about their quest for a holy war and their mission of kicking foreign invaders our of their motherland.

"Government and foreign forces control very little inside Afghanistan," mentioned another relative. They sounded so sure about their statements and had no fear of talking badly about the corrupt current regime. As far as the United States and allies were concerned, my companions simply shook their heads and would say only that they were in the area for their own benefit.

"They are wasting their money and people," one man offered, saying that Americans would learn their lesson, just as the Russians had. I felt devastated, as this was not what I had expected to hear. I had thought the people of Afghanistan would feel differently about the American and NATO presence. I started to ask more direct questions about why they were comparing the United States's fate to the Russians'. They were very quick to point out that billions of U.S. dollars and resources had been falling into the wrong hands and that millions of innocent people all around the country did not benefit from foreigners' presence and support. Abdul Rahim was even more vocal, challenging me to simply look at these villages and surroundings to see if a single about them had changed since my last time here. He pointed out that not a single school had been built inside Arghandi, though it was only eighteen kilometers from the capital, Kabul.

By now, I was starting to establish a good grasp of how and why opposing factions and Taliban forces continued to grow inside Afghanistan and how disappointed the innocent people in and around Kabul felt about the direction their devastated and oppressed nation was heading in.

# Kabul the Filthy City

IT WAS TIME TO EXPLORE KABUL, the city that had been the darling of tourists from the early 1950s until the late '70s. I had been
warned to be extremely careful about my movement in Kabul. I
had called upon my late brother's trusted friend and a former freedom fighter, Aziz, to take me around. I was ready for a big day of
discovery; I was in search of truth and the impact of devastating wars,
corruption, and waste. Aziz had promised to take me to my old
neighborhood, Shahrara. He had been Zia's best friend, and had
fought alongside him for many years against Russian forces and
the communist regime. He had been hurting badly since my brother's
death, and had asked to spend time with me during my visit.

I was well prepared for a big day of touring and filming. Aziz had
no problem with my camera work, but warned me to be careful
when encountering military zones, and particularly U.S. and other
NATO forces, on the way.

Minutes away from the hotel, I started to notice a mix of very
old buildings and a ton of new constructions painted in bright,
ugly colors. "Where do these colors come from?" I asked.

"None of these are built according to code; they have no proper sewer system or solid foundations. People just bribe their way to building them. And these are not traditional Afghan colors, they are Pakistani colors. Everything gets imported, even our colors, now," Aziz said, his voice full of disappointment.

"What happened to Zarnegar Park?" I asked Aziz about Kabul's most famous central park, which has been the site to many big demonstrations and had become the epicenter of many parties opposing the kingdom during the early years of revolt. The park was also an excellent place for recreation; hundreds of people, including Afghan army soldiers, would pack the site during their days off. Now, I could see only a little bit of the park; it seemed crowded with buildings, and even had a big mosque inside it.

"It is a beautiful mosque, but why did they build it inside the historical park?" I asked.

"Well, someone paid a huge amount of money and built it right in the middle of the park," Aziz said. Building a mosque, of course, is always seen as a very respectful and proper action by Muslim communities around the world, so we knew it was a sensitive matter, but we were baffled by why anyone would have built it in such a crowded area, without any parking or easy access. "It is indeed very disappointing," Aziz confirmed. "It is a beautiful mosque capable of accommodating many people, but to put it right in the middle of a historical place is quite shocking—but, well, with money you can buy anything here."

We drove through extremely busy and filthy streets, with no marked lanes or directions, filled with thousands of slow-moving cars, fruit carts, and people. Within minutes there were at least five young boys and girls moving alongside the car, extending their hands toward the window and begging for money.

"Please don't give them money," Aziz told me.

"How can I not? " I asked him.

"I know exactly how you feel, but soon there will be hundreds of them," he explained

"They are glued to the car, Aziz—I am afraid they will get hurt," I said.

"They are so used to moving closely, and I honestly have not seen any get hurt so far, thank God," he sighed.

I stopped filming at that point, as I did not see any benefit in it, and, more important, it would signal that I was a visitor. I was heartbroken to see hundreds of beautiful young kids making their way between the cars and on the sidelines, begging for money and food.

"This is what drives people crazy," Aziz said. "This city is made for no more than three hundred thousand people, but we now have five million in it." Of those who live in Kabul, he added, three-quarters live in poverty.

"This is the result of money falling into the wrong hands," he concluded, and explained to me that this whole city of over five million people was entirely controlled by probably a couple hundred warlords and millionaires.

We struggled for a good half hour before we made it to the front of the Kabul municipal building and ministry of education and onto the Salang Watt, the highway named after Afghanistan's famous mountain. We were moving across the Shahrara area, which used to be nothing but empty land and meadows but was now filled with stores and ugly high-rise buildings, most of which were walled in with ugly-colored glass. These mega buildings just did not fit well with the makeup of a half-demolished city full of very old and broken structures.

"With no sewer system in place, how in the world do they allow these constructions to continue?" I asked Aziz.

"Well, it is all about filthy money and lack of planning," he replied, explaining that the current government did not care about ordinary people, and that it was all about the few who held all the wealth.

After another half-hour drive, we had just made our way to the opposite side of the old fruit market, which was only a few hundred feet away from our home, when Aziz suddenly pulled his cell phone and called someone.

"We are coming in," he told the person on the other end of the line.

"I think you will be happy to see a very good friend of your family," he told me as he instructed the driver to continue through the old fruit market area, which looked way different from how it had in years past.

"Look at him," he said, pointing to a gray-haired, bearded man.

"Oh my God!" I yelled. "This is Shah Mahmood, the famous neighborhood boy!"

"Yep, that is him. He is the only one from his big family left in this area."

I anxiously got out of the car and stood in front of Shah Mahmood. He did not recognize me at first, but within seconds he ran toward me and started crying. We hugged for a long time as we cried and cried, without saying much.

"I am so sorry about Ziaullah. I truly miss him; he was my hero," he said, as he started talking about my brother, with whom Shah had been very close and who had spent numerous days and nights at Shah's home and store in this area during the war years.

"I used to house him all the time and hide him from government and Russian forces," Shah told us. He then pointed to a hidden underground location and said he had hidden my brother and several freedom fighters there many times.

"How come you are the only one here? Why didn't you join the rest of your family in the United States and Europe?" I asked him.

He told us that he had made a decision to live his life right where he was. He said his lot where his business/home was was now worth $1 million, but he would rather live his remaining life right there.

"A million dollars?" I asked him.

"Yes, probably even a little more than that—it is a prime location—but I want to keep it till I die," Shah answered. He informed me that he had lived in the same location for the last thirty-five years, despite some very tough times of abuse and hardship. He said he was very happy to take care of his friends and make his space available to all.

Soon, we were sitting around on the floor with at least ten other men from Shahrara who had found out about my visit. I was very happy to see so many old friends but sad to find them looking so weary and old. Even my younger former soccer teammates looked so much older than their age, and most had gray hair. Tired and weary, they all talked about their struggles and loss of many friends and family members throughout the years, but proudly described having stuck around the neighborhood and made it through. They even joked about some difficult times when they had had to hide in each other's basements. One friend laughed loudly as he talked about not being able to go to the bathroom for more than fourteen hours because of neighborhood home searches one day. Another man talked about hiding inside a chimney for more than six hours one night after a search by Russian troops.

After an emotional visit with the boys from the old neighborhood, it was time to go see my old home. As we turned around the famous women's park and onto the old Shahrara road, which was unpaved and badly beaten, the car started shaking from side to side as it went over the bumps and potholes. The recent snow and cold had created even more difficulty for drivers and pedestrians.

"My God, there is the old fish store!" I yelled as I looked to my right to find the blackened storefront, which looked like it had not been touched for the last thirty years. "Yes, it was open 'til recently," Aziz said.

I turned on the camera and told Aziz that I was not going to turn it off until we were out of Shahrara.

"Okay, that is fine, but just remember, it is no longer the same place. Most of Shahrara is dominated by real bad people—famous thugs and kidnappers. The area is very dangerous, so try to hide the camera as much as possible," he said. "I am going to move as slowly as I can, but I will not stop, as you will see very curious gang members and thugs just standing around."

I told him that I would just keep rolling the camera and would appreciate his slowing down as much as possible once we were in front of my old house.

We moved toward old Shahrara, and I noticed the big old garage that used to be the main bus station from which people would depart to the northern part of the country. Its door, which resembled an ancient fort's gate, still stood there as if no one had touched it. A flurry of activity was happening in and around it.

"Wow, they used to bomb this one a lot. How come the walls are still standing?" I asked Aziz as we passed the old military depot. "They must have missed its strong walls," he said, and laughed.

The area along the entire long wall of the depot was covered in garbage.

"They don't even clean the area around a military base?" I asked.

"Well, they really don't care," Aziz said. "God knows what is going on inside; it is filthy all around," he continued with frustration.

# Lost Decency

I pointed my camera up and down the road, turning from side to side. Within minutes we were at the gate of the base, but realized they had permanently shut the door on this side, allowing all the neighborhood garbage to pile up behind it. We did not dare to open the windows, but saw a ton of residents simply move by despite the bad odor.

"Wow, these poor people now seem to be completely immunized against germs," I said.

"Oh, yes! We are now germ-resistant. It is not just this area," Aziz replied. "The whole city is full of garbage."

"But doesn't this concern the government and municipalities? We get billions of dollars in U.S. and foreign aid; you would think this would be a priority," I remarked.

"Atta, get real—the country is controlled by thugs and vicious warlords. This government and everyone else knows it," Aziz said. "Afghanistan has turned into a jungle—there is no rule, it is all about getting rich and nothing here for the ordinary people."

Despite not many changes in construction in the area, the street seemed so much tighter; everything looked small, beaten up, and extremely dirty, with the typical look of a war-torn zone, and the people looked desperate and destitute.

"Please stop," I asked the driver as we approached the alley where my family's home was. He pulled the car aside and asked me not to get out.

I realized I was in tears and did not know what to say, so I just kept on filming, pointing the camera toward the alley and my home. The structure remained intact but looked like it had been renovated a little on the outside.

"We could knock on the door and potentially go inside," Aziz suggested.

"No, I am not interested," I told him. I did not want to go in there; I felt devastated and just wanted to move on.

As we drove away, I filmed Shahrara's entire main road and its surroundings, all the way to Burj Shahrara, a historic tower built hundreds of years earlier. The bright-colored brick tower was still standing and looked very much the same as it had thirty years ago. I asked Aziz to stop the car so that I could walk closer. I wanted to touch the wall and lean against the mighty old tower again. I remembered gathering for years with my soccer teammates below this tower, before almost all our soccer matches and group marches. I felt weaker and weaker as I wept for a long time, until Aziz took my hand and led me back inside the car. He had been planning to show me more of Kabul, but I was no longer in the mood to see it. I just wanted to think about the past and the lovely, peaceful, innocent, and simple way of life, without any fear, that we had once enjoyed in our homeland.

# Corrupt Dinner

ОNE OF MY BIGGEST PLANS during my visit was to go to my old workplace, the Hotel Inter-Continental, but I found out upon my arrival that the new members of parliament were all staying there for safety reasons as a result of disapproval from the Afghan president. We heard the president was not happy with the new session because of the selection of several members from opposing political parties, who had allegedly committed fraud by paying millions to get elected.

I asked my friend Ahmad to find a way for us to visit anyway. A young, successful cousin of his knew a prominent member of the parliament and agreed to arrange it for us. After a couple of days, we got a call that it was all set.

"I am happy, as I would hate to not visit my famous former workplace," I told Ahmad.

"He wants us to dress in suits and ties," he said.

The next evening, Ahmad's cousin Sarwar and his uniformed bodyguard, equipped with a machine gun, came to pick us up from our hotel right after sunset. He told Ahmad and me to get in the backseat, while he posed as our driver.

"Remember, you are members of parliament!" he told us, looking us right in the eye.

"What are you talking about?" I asked.

"This is awesome, Atta—we just got promoted!" Ahmad seemed so happy, as if he truly had gotten a promotion. I was more skeptical, though; I had no idea what Sarwar had in mind.

The bodyguard started driving really fast, despite lots of traffic all around us.

"Can you slow down a little?" Ahmad asked.

"I can't—I must drive fast today," the bodyguard mentioned with a smirk.

We then realized it was more of a security matter, as a car with armed personnel would be too visible and an easy target, so we held on to our door handles and strapped our seat belts tight. It was a very scary pace for the unregulated and chaotic streets of Kabul, as our driver maneuvered his way in and out of concrete barriers, but we figured he knew exactly how to get around.

We then drove toward the northern part of city and through the Bagh-e Bala High garden area, where we started to see hotel lights displayed beautifully on top of the hill in the distance.

"Remember what I told you!" yelled Sarwar as he pulled inside the entrance gate of the Hotel Inter-Continental, where dozens of armored cars were parked and thirty or forty security personnel were standing around, holding heavy machine guns and gear.

"We never had a real gate before," I said.

"Now you have two," Sarwar said. "And we are going to go through a full security checkpoint later, at the top of the hill. By the way, don't talk to any security personnel here or upstairs," he warned us.

As the car came to a full stop, some armed guards approached and the bodyguard rolled down his window.

*"Wakil sahebastan,"* ("they are parliament members") he said, while looking back at us. The officer peeked inside and saw Ahmad and me. We just looked at him.

"Your guard must get out of the car," the officer informed Sarwar.

Within seconds, the gate swung upon and we drove up the hill toward the hotel.

*"Wakil Sahib* ['Mr. Representative'], how are you?" Ahmad started joking around as he looked at me. It all sounded very funny, but it wasn't really a laughing matter, I thought. What if we got caught?

"Don't worry, you will be a *wakil* [the official name of parliament members] for two more minutes, but once inside the hotel, you are Atta," he said. I then realized we were being referred to as *wakils* only to get past the security gates and gain access to the hotel.

"What a relief," I told them. I said I honestly did not want to go inside and still pretend to be a parliament member.

We pulled into the hotel parking lot, which was filled with luxury cars and security guards—a bizarre scene of luxury and military presence. I quickly remembered the time when only a few cars had been parked there; the majority of this space had been used to showcase the Afghan national dance *(atan)* in the middle, surrounded by beautiful flowers representing various parts of the country, but it now looked like a military complex. I honestly could not remember ever having seen this many armed personnel and weapons in front of this hotel, even during local communist or Russian rule.

Armed guards led us to the security checkpoint, which had been built on the hillside that used to be a very nice pathway to the swimming pool and tennis courts. There was now an ugly, trailer-type room equipped with body and luggage scanners and attended by several armed security guards.

"What is this?" asked one guard, pointing to the camcorder that I laid in front of them. I told them it was a camera; he asked me to turn it on. The guard first looked puzzled but somehow was impressed with our appearance and did not question me further.

"Please be careful to not film any members of the parliament," Sarwar said. I told him that I would not film anyone, but would just take a few photos of the place, if appropriate and away from everyone's eyes, as we entered the hotel lobby.

"Oh my God," I sighed.

"What?" asked Ahmad.

"What a shame! Everything looks so ugly," I remarked as I viewed the concierge and lobby area. The once immaculate five-star hotel, which had been one of the top five hotels in Asia and a place people dreamed of visiting, now looked filthy, with ugly colors.

We slowly made our way through the lobby, which was jampacked with parliament representatives and their families. The scene reminded me of the night of the Russian invasion, when the lobby had been filled with panicked foreigners and journalists, except now it was occupied by our own happy members of parliament, wearing a variety of civil and traditional dress.

"Don't you think our parliament members should have been required to put on suits?" I asked. "Look at these people's appearance—they look so unprofessional! I love our traditional uniforms, but this is not what our nation needs. This is more like a traditional-fashion show."

We then realized that most people in the lobby were watching us, since we were dressed in suits and ties and by far looked more professional and formal than all of them.

"Why are there so many women and children around?" I asked Sarwar.

"Well, as you know, the parliament is in limbo, so they have been meeting here for a whole week," he said as we kept walking toward the hotel restaurant, where we were to meet with a friend of Sarwar's, a prominent member of Afghan parliament and an influential figure from the north of the country. As we got closer to the end of the lobby, we noticed a group of about thirty women and children gathered right in front of the hotel elevators. I then realized the entrance to a beautiful restaurant had been sealed, and a former banquet hall had instead become the main restaurant, which looked packed as we waited.

Within about five minutes, Ahmad's cousin appeared with a hotel employee dressed in a suit, who asked us to follow him through the crowded restaurant and all the way to the end, where we spotted a man surrounded by a few other men dressed in traditional Afghan garb. We were introduced to the man at the head of the table, so we knew this was the man from the north. He was very pleasant as he greeted us, and the other men emptied their chairs and left. We apologized for interrupting their lavish dinner; the table was covered with kabobs and various other dishes. While Ahmad kept on socializing and talking, I was more concerned with the environment and people around me. I realized I was acting like a lost child inside a park, just looking for someone to help me.

I was mainly mad about the whole situation. I was now associating with a prominent member of the parliament and witnessing up close the caliber of individuals responsible for the future of our homeland. As we started talking about life in the United States, I quickly realized the parliament member had actually traveled there on numerous occasions and knew about quite a few states and places. I wondered

# Atta Arghandiwal

how he had managed those trips, until I learned that the majority of these representatives had been war commanders with deep pockets or members of their families had purchased their votes in their areas. I was later told that quite a few of these officials traveled around the world regularly.

"I am so sorry, but I have to go out for a few minutes," said the parliament member, after a man came and whispered in his ear. We noticed many other parliament members leaving the restaurant, too.

"There is actually a fight in the lobby," said the waiter. I stood up and told them that I was going to get some food from the buffet table. I was very tempted to take my camcorder with me but realized it was not appropriate in the presence of all these important people, so I went to grab a plate and stood off to the side of the buffet table, pretending I was waiting to get food. I walked closer to the entrance and saw a huge crowd of parliament representatives yelling and screaming at each other and some pulling others away from the scene.

"What really happened?" I asked the waiter in front of the buffet table.

"They beat up a representative," he said. "It was a fight between a Hazara and a Pashtun rep first, and then the ladies got into it."

By then the whole area was in chaos, as parliament representatives and security personnel filled the lobby area. The prominent parliament member from our table returned to the restaurant after about forty-five minutes, looking tired and embarrassed. He told us there had been a little struggle between couples and that he had had to intervene. He told us that the women and children sitting one table away from us were actually members of his family and had come to visit him from the north. I then looked around and realized that

*268*

about twelve members of his family were busy with their lavish meals and staying at the hotel, at the expense of poor Afghan people.

"Wow, it is so disgusting—they have no shame about their lifestyle and abuse of power," I mentioned to Ahmad after dinner.

"This is nothing, Atta; this is just pocket change. You have no idea how much money a man like this one has now. He is filthy rich," he said.

"But I thought these officials get paid a very small amount," I said.

"It is not about their salary; most of these warlords have spent millions of dollars to buy their seats," Ahmad replied.

You need to spend more time learning about Afghanistan and what happens to billions of dollars here," Sarwar remarked.

Sad and very disappointed, I walked around the hotel lobby and then down to my old office area. I stood in front of my closed office for a few minutes with tears running down my cheeks as I remembered the good old days of peace and promise in this country that was now in the hands of an unqualified and vicious few.

# Party People

DESPITE OUR VERY BUSY SCHEDULE, Ahmad and I quickly became acquainted with several elite members of the government and private sector during our stay at the Kabul Serena Hotel.

As newcomers who looked like businessmen, we were watched every step of the way. Everyone tried to get close to us so they could learn about our motive for being here and our plans during our trip. As a result of these interactions, I also learned that various parties with financial and professional power were very close to each other and liked to party together.

While the majority of people in Afghanistan today suffer from the effects of decades of war, devastation, and poverty, the corrupt members of government and the elite with access to money and resources throw lavish celebrations like there is no tomorrow. These parties happen all week long—weekends no longer mean anything special. Ahmad and I were asked to join a dinner or a party every day, sometimes multiple times. We participated hesitantly in a few of these events; although I always felt guilty about it, I was also curious to learn about these people's shamelessly extravagant lifestyle.

Two days before our departure from Kabul, Ahmad returned from a coffee meeting with some businessmen and said, "You are going to meet some very important people tonight."

"You mean, we are going to see some of these corrupt guys up close?" I asked.

"Yes, but no cameras or photos, please," he laughed.

"But how did you just get invited? Do you know them very well?" I asked

"They don't care; they are just interested in our ideas."

"I don't mind going—I want to know what's going on—but what about me? Did you tell them about me?" I asked.

"You are in for a treat," was all Ahmad would say.

"But they hardly know us. Isn't this crazy?" I asked.

"You are going to be safe, but in the company of the corrupt for a night!" he said with a smile. "Don't you want to learn more about them?"

"Of course I do—these people are treating us like kings—but how in the world did you establish such a close relationship with these people?" I asked.

"I honestly just share my ideas and wish to help but have no interest or ownership in their moneymaking. I just want to make a difference," Ahmad explained. I knew he always wished to be of service to his own people by using his great ideas and extensive background in financial services, but I simply wanted him to be careful of rampant corruption, as well as protect his personal safety.

"Do you know where we are going tonight?" I asked him.

"Not really, but I know it is in the Shar-e Naw area. We will take a cab there and have the driver pick us up again later," he said.

"This is real Mafia stuff," I commented.

"Well, then, let's make sure we dress properly, too," Ahmad responded, with a smirk on his face.

Ahmad instructed the taxi driver to take us behind the Haji Yaqoub mosque and stop in front of a supermarket. We sat inside the cab for a good ten minutes, until someone knocked on the side window of the car. Ahmad rolled down the window, and the armed man stated my friend's last name. We paid the cab driver and followed the man for a few feet before he asked us to get into a brand-new Land Cruiser.

"We have a short drive to the house, only minutes away," said the security guard. The car drove away in a hurry and entered an alley in Shar-e Naw, turning onto a bumpy, unpaved road. Within five minutes or so, the car pulled up in front of a house guarded by at least ten armed men, with cement blocks closing parts of the alley to prevent speeding cars from passing through.

We were then led into the house through a big metal door. Right at the entrance was a small room with a security scanner; we went through a thorough body scan and then were taken to a big yard. "My goodness," I sighed, as I spotted a mansion across the lawn. I started to worry a little when I realized only a small portion of the house was lit.

After we went through another security check, two young men led us toward the megahome, as I wondered why we were walking into a dark house. After a couple hundred feet, we encountered some construction on our left, which looked like rooms filled with office furniture and computers. We passed these offices and the big house on our right and approached a small room right in the middle of the yard. As we got closer, we realized it was actually an entry to an underground area. Ahmad and I looked at each other with concern; I thought we were in big trouble.

# Lost Decency

"*Befarmayain* ['welcome']. Go in," one of the young men said politely, as he swung the door open and onto a stairway. Ahmad and I looked at each other, puzzled and alarmed. I asked Ahmad to go first, as I knew I would not recognize anyone down there and we had no idea where we were heading. As we descended the well-lit cement stairs, we passed light-colored walls and finally stepped down into an entryway decorated nicely with modern furniture and large Afghan rugs.

"Oh, *salaam, salaam,*" said two men as they came to greet us with firm hugs, as though we were old friends reuniting after a long time.

We walked into a huge party room where at least fifty people sat. Beyond a big bar were a large dinner table and a pool table at the other end of the room. As was customary, we started shaking hands with everyone inside the room, as each person stood and politely exchanged greetings with us.

"We will introduce everyone later one by one," yelled the man in charge.

It was obvious that we were welcome and recognized as guests and newcomers from outside of Afghanistan, as each person politely offered their seat. Everyone seemed extremely friendly as we started to converse with many people around the room. From the look of people, it seemed that there were many government and private businesspeople at the party, so I was very anxious to find out who they were and learn about the inner circles of Afghan society.

Within half an hour the host stood up to introduce all the guests. He completely surprised everybody with how much he knew about each person, as he talked about their position, the nature of their business, and even their ethnic origin. He proudly announced that the party that night represented every single ethnic group in Afghanistan. That was truly a welcome statement, despite the unpleasant and uncomfortable feelings I had about this elite gathering.

We soon found out that we were actually sitting with some of the most corrupt and dangerous men controlling Kabul and probably the entire country, including first and second deputy ministers, heads of security agencies, and at least two high-ranking banking officials.

When our turn to introduce ourselves came, I was very hesitant but also wanted the group to know who Ahmad and I were. Both of us had been very fortunate to have established great careers and extensive experience in the area of financial services, as well as leadership development, so the crowd was extremely interested to find out more about us and started asking questions. It seemed like the crowd stopped even being interested in hearing anything more about the other partygoers, as the focus remained on both of us. It was an intriguing moment, as I was curious to know what they thought of the talent that existed outside of Afghanistan.

"Hope you are here to stay!" one prominent official yelled.

"Welcome! We are so happy to have you here tonight," said another.

These introductions were followed by a huge feast. A group of five or six young men flooded the table with various dishes, and as I approached to get a plate, the host stopped me. "We are honored to have you guys here," he said.

"Many thanks. We are very happy to be here," I told him.

When I sat next to Ahmad to eat my dinner, I asked him, "Who are all these people?"

"Well, these are lots of dangerous people, from every party of the past and present you can think of," he answered.

"Okay, then let's talk later—this place is wired! Look around," I said.

# Lost Decency

We both started looking around the room and at the corners of the ceiling and noticed several visible cameras, which did not make sense, I thought. Why would they reveal the cameras so openly? I wondered. But I realized Ahmad and I were the only two strangers in the room—everyone else here was close and friendly with one another.

"Let's go inside the big house for music!" yelled the host after dinner, as he guided the guests up the stairs and into the big house. It had multiple floors and a huge living room furnished with lavish sofas, bright Afghan carpets, and tables. Chandeliers hung in various areas. Two musicians were stationed in the corner on mattresses covered with rugs.

"You have to be careful, Ahmad," I told my friend, after we got a ride back to our hotel from the host. I advised Ahmad not to get too close, but rather to work with these people only when he had to, without getting involved in their nasty dealings.

"I am not doing anything illegal—I am an honest businessman," he retorted. "But they are all trying very hard to get closer and closer to me, and it is making me very uncomfortable," he admitted.

His confession saddened and angered me. I asked Ahmad if this was a one-of-a-kind party or a frequent type of event. He told me that Kabul had indeed turned into a big party city for the filthy rich, and indicated that this type of gathering took place almost seven days a week, so that those people with money and power could negotiate business deals and establish new connections. As I thought back on all the people I had seen at the underground party, Ahmad's explanation made more sense: I had witnessed many slick personalities from various backgrounds and races who were very comfortable with each other—and none of them seemed to care about the innocent and needy.

# Atta Arghandiwal

Despite my frustration about the obvious lack of care for the ordinary by elite and corrupt officials, I was happy to have witnessed such a party with my own eyes, as it allowed me to establish a better understanding of my beloved homeland and empathy for its innocent people. As a devout Afghan, I had been following the events in my country since the day I left and had been particularly interested to learn more about the current government and the United States's and allies' role in Afghanistan's future. As a matter of fact, I had been thinking of trying to help my native country in some capacity since 9/11, but now I realized that thousands of Afghanis around the world, despite their extensive skills and knowledge, have no room within this corrupt environment.

In the days ahead, I inquired and learned more and more about the suffering and disappointment of innocent people and the lack of any true progress in Afghanistan, despite the flow of billions of U.S. and allies' dollars and vast resources. As much as I felt terrible for the ordinary people living inside Afghanistan who had been put at such a disadvantage, though, I was happy for and proud of the lucky ones, including my entire family, who had made it to the United States, Europe, and other countries around the world that live in peace and prosperity and offer a promising future for the generations to come.

# Closing Thoughts

As a result of failed policies, major shifts, and forced changes, combined with the incompetence of local Afghan government officials, Afghanistan has witnessed massive violent confrontations that have dominated the political and social environment of the country over the course of last four decades. This has caused over two million deaths while forcing over seven million Afghanis into exile—not to mention the massive destruction of farms and livestock, forced economic system changes, and a dependency on foreign aid.

A proud people and country, once the darling of western tourism, is no more. Afghanistan was not always like this. From the early '50s into late '60s and early '70s, it was a country making progress. Afghan women pursued advanced education and built careers alongside men. There was law and order, and the government took on massive projects such as hydropower infrastructure and other national endeavors. Forty years ago, Kabul was considered the playground of Central Asia, a city where girls wore jeans to school and to university.

After the Soviet troops' defeat and ultimate departure from Afghanistan in 1989, along with the loss of millions of people and many more thousands who were maimed or who suffered from displacement and humiliation in the refugee camps, the innocent people of Afghanistan dreamed of participating in the country's reconstruction and living in peace and dignity. But lack of interest and coordination by the UN and Western nations allowed the warring factions within Afghanistan to start a civil war that would soon destroys any dreams the Afghan people may have had for the restoration of peace, stability, and communal security.

Years of neglect by the international community, including by the U.S., which had been the most powerful supporter of Afghan resistance against communism and the Russian invasion, created a power vacuum. Ordinary Afghans did not have the resources to put the country back on its feet again, making it extremely vulnerable to interference from neighboring countries, especially Pakistan and Iran, and ultimately resulting in the rise of the Taliban.

Non-Afghans and other outlaws in Middle East, led by Osama bin Laden, used Afghanistan's territories consistently to execute vicious plans to secure residency. They used violence and military power against locals, and broke the traditional norms of Afghan civil society with violence.

When the United States and their allies went to war in Afghanistan in 2001—with the aim of removing the safe haven that the Taliban had provided for Al-Qaeda—it was widely hoped that innocent Afghans would be liberated from a regime that denied them education, jobs, and other basic needs. But the focus and energy was on the costly war in Iraq. While one hundred thousand troops were sent to Iraq, only seventeen thousand were sent to Afghanistan. This was during a time when the Taliban and other non-Afghan fighters were on the run. The United States and its allies made a colossal mistake by allowing various warring factions and their leaders to take control of key parts of the country while their own resources were diverted elsewhere. Ultimately, most of the country fell once again into the hands of the same warlords responsible for previous atrocities.

Millions of innocent Afghans, tired and weary of decades of despair of war, wished and hoped for peace, for a light at the end of the tunnel. But the U.S. and its allies instead installed the incompetent Karzai regime. Without a clear vision for securing the country and eliminating the rules of the warlords, the U.S. and its allies lost a golden opportunity to help build a national army capable of securing and defending Afghanistan and a government that would focus on education, agriculture, and other basic human needs.

With millions of U.S. dollars and foreign aid flowing into the hands of the incompetent central government, a Mafia-style operation developed within the country. I remember being struck by a statement made by a senior U.S. commander in which he implied that corruption was part of the Afghan culture. I wanted to tell the world that he was wrong, that corruption had never been part of the Afghan culture before; that it had only started since 9/11, since the implementation of bad policies, and since the country had been run over by scores of former warlords. The Mafia-style government resulted in the growth of various militias by controlling the flow of money, hiring foreign security firms, and opening the trade and sale of government and NGO contracts. Millions of dollars in contracts have been privately trading hands for resale through private hands for over ten years.

The production and trade of opium through the hands of many of these same warlords has become another embarrassing issue for the Afghan people. It is believed that Afghanistan is the world's largest producer of opium and drugs. As a result, predatory corruption, fueled by booming a narcotics industry, is rampant at various levels, both inside the government and privately. I remember a friend asking, "Aren't we capable of reading license plates through GPS? How come we don't see massive opium fields all across Afghanistan? Can't we just destroy them?" I replied that it would quite easy for the United States to do so, but that has never been part of the plan. Large sums of cash have been wired out of Afghanistan into the Middle East, European cities, and even back to the U.S. Many warlords and government officials have invested in mansions and large commercial real estate deals in prominent parts of Dubai and other safe havens that have become home to many Afghan officials as they continue to secure and keep their wealth away from Afghanistan.

Ironic how the world used to see Afghanistan as a patriotic nation, even a nation with power and resilience, but now it's seen as one of the world's most dangerous spots and is associated with the word "terrorism." But who are we to blame?

While all the people of Afghanistan have suffered a lot during the last few decades, innocent women and children are the primary victims. In human terms, Afghanistan is one of the poorest and most miserable countries in the world. Life expectancy is about forty-six years, which is among the lowest in the world. One in six Afghan children will die before their fifth birthday, and half of those who survive suffer from chronic malnutrition. There are almost two million widows out of an estimated population of twenty-seven million. Over 90 percent of Afghan widows have children. Shelter, food, making a living, and social protection are the most pressing challenges for widows in Afghanistan.

# Lost Decency

Women, but particularly widows, face great challenges because of exclusion, forced marriages, gender-based violence, and lack of education and economic opportunities. Unlike the old days, when society protected widows, today the death of a husband means that their surviving wives lack any economic independence. They receive no social protection due to greed and a renewed sense of individualism. While there are glimpses of hope in the form of representation of women in parliament and some other government and private industries, women largely do not have a voice to express their problems. They continue to be deprived of meaningful representation in social institutions.

Many Afghans, meanwhile, have been lucky enough to have run away from the despair of war and death at the hands of invaders, and to have transitioned from refugee status to bona fide citizens of countries around the world. They've made remarkable adjustments by assimilating themselves into their new homes and cultures. These are musicians and artists, professional athletes and scientists, law enforcement officers, and computer scientists. They've been able to boost the wealth of their chosen nation's talents while sadly depriving their homeland of their valuable human assets.

Today, the entire Afghanistan establishment is superfluous; it's a very expensive solution to what could have been a small problem. The United States and its allies had a great opportunity after 9/11 to build a model and to show the rest of the world what it would have looked like to come to the aid of a country victimized and traumatized by war.

Afghanistan today is faced today with an unenviable future filled with numerous challenges, including widespread corruption, drug trafficking, injustices, and poverty. Rampant corruption continues to prevent any improvement that might otherwise happen. But what if Afghanistan had remained just a stop on the "hippie trail"? What if the Soviet Union had never invaded? What if Afghanistan had never been deserted after Russian withdrawal? Do you think 9/11 would have happened?

When all said and done, what's been allowed to happen is a loss of decency. The majority of the population of millions of decent Afghans had nothing to do with the policies and forced changes that have affected their country. Once-proud Afghans have come to realize that what we see and hear is not real, but only an illusion.

But there are times when we look deep into our souls and the mirror of our hearts and we see a reflection that is our true selves. What we see and feel in that reflection is a wound that has never been healed. A painful wound, as our hearts bleed for our country and our innocent people. In that reflection we see our people and it's hard to recognize them. We may ask, "Where are our beautiful sisters and brothers?" But there is no answer, only silence.

# Acknowledgments

To Deborah Buchta, for the great introduction to one of the best literary coaches I could have found. To Brooke Warner at Warner Coaching, my coach and editor, for her great knowledge and mentorship. She was the person to put my book on the right track. To Annie Tucker, for her amazing eye and for making my work shine. To Lydia D'moch, my creative book designer. To my amazing big family and their help to recall these true stories and wonders. To Anil Whadhwani, for his ongoing motivation and support. To Asghar Nowrouz, for his valuable input and ongoing support.

# About the Author

ATTA ARGHANDIWAL was born in Afghanistan but has spent over half of his life in the West. As one of ten kids within a large military family, Arghandiwal spent much of his young life traveling and attending school in various parts of the country.

Shortly after graduating from high school, Arghandiwal joined the Afghan Air Force to finish his military assignment. After witnessing unexpected political changes, beginning with the 1978 communist coup d'etat, and ultimately leading to the invasion by the Soviet Union, Arghandiwal left his home country in August of 1980 and became a refugee in Germany. He immigrated to the United States in December 1981, where he went on to build a successful banking career.

With deep passion and pride in his heritage, Arghandiwal has written the true Afghan story in order to increase awareness about his country's political upheaval and the innocent people who have been caught in the chaos. He has remained an independent banking consultant while attending to his lifetime passion of writing.

Arghandiwal is married and lives with his wife and two children in Northern California.